Editor
Eric Migliaccio

Editorial Project Manager
Ina Massler Levin, M.A.

Editor in Chief
Sharon Coan, M.S. Ed.

Illustrator
Denice Adorno

Cover Artist
Jessica Orlando

Art Coordinator
Denice Adorno

Creative Director
Elayne Roberts

Imaging
Alfred Lau
Ralph Olmedo, Jr.

Product Manager
Phil Garcia

Publishers
Rachelle Cracchiolo, M.S. Ed.
Mary Dupuy Smith, M.S. Ed.

Expository Writing

Grades 3–5

Written by

Robert Summers

Teacher Created Materials, Inc.
6421 Industry Way
Westminster, CA 92683
www.teachercreated.com
ISBN-1-57690-989-1
©2000 Teacher Created Materials, Inc.
Made in U.S.A.

The classroom teacher may reproduce copies of materials in this book for classroom use only. The reproduction of any part for an entire school or school system is strictly prohibited. No part of this publication may be transmitted, stored, or recorded in any form without written permission from the publisher.

Table of Contents

Introduction 5

Standards for Writing (Intermediate) 6

The Expository-Writing Rubric 10

Four-Point Writing Rubric 11

Create Your Own Rubric 12

The Basics of Punctuation 14

Editing Marks 19

The Components of Expository Writing 20

What Is Expository Writing? 21

    Worksheet #1 24

    Worksheet #2 25

    Worksheet #3 26

The Writing Process 28

    Worksheet #1 31

    Worksheet #2 32

    Thank-You Note Frame 33

Paragraph Perfection 34

    Worksheet #1 36

    Worksheet #2 37

Terrific Topic Sentences 39

    The Four Types of Sentences 41

    End Punctuation 41

    Worksheet #1 42

    Worksheet #2 43

Superb Summaries 44

    Guidelines for Writing a Summary 46

    Worksheet #1 47

    Worksheet #2 48

Table of Contents *(cont.)*

Parts of Speech 50
Nifty Nouns and Vivid Verbs 51
    Nifty Nouns Worksheet. 53
    Vivid Verbs Worksheet 54
Adjective Attention. 55
    Worksheet. 57
Appealing Adverbs 58
    Worksheet. 60

Figurative Language 62
Simile Spice 63
    Worksheet. 65
Marvelous Metaphors 66
    How to Address an Envelope. 69
    How to Write a Friendly Letter 69
    Worksheet. 70
Personification Motivation 71
    Worksheet. 74

Types of Paragraphs 76
The Explanatory Paragraph. 77
    Guidelines for Writing an Explanatory Paragraph 80
    Worksheet. 81
Writing Directions 83
    Common Rules to Follow When Writing or Giving Directions 86
    Worksheet. 87
    The Cause-and-Effect Paragraph 88
    Worksheet #1 91
    Worksheet #2 93
The Contrast Paragraph 94
    Worksheet. 96
The Comparison Paragraph. 97
    Worksheet. 100

Table of Contents *(cont.)*

Using References 101

Thesaurus Power 102

    Worksheet 104

The Atlas and the Almanac 106

    Worksheet 108

    Mapping Criteria Sheet 110

Parts of a Book 111

    Worksheet 115

Skimming and Scanning 116

    Worksheet 119

Creating Reports 121

Book Report Form 122

Outrageous Outlines 123

    Sample Outline 126

    Worksheet #1 127

    Worksheet #2 128

    Worksheet #3 130

The Research Report 132

    How to Write a Bibliography 135

    Sample Composition 136

Answer Key 137

Introduction

Expository writing is writing for real purposes and real audiences. These compositions must be expressive and descriptive while also being informative and instructive. Whether the paragraphs explain a simple procedure or provide detailed descriptions of people, places, objects, or experiences, an author has to carefully plan, research, organize, and revise the material before it is published. A main idea is presented and supported with appropriate facts and background information that must maintain the reader's interest. The expository paragraph serves as a foundation of nonfiction—not fantasy and role-playing. This type of writing is the one most commonly required in school, yet it is often the most difficult for students to master. The purpose of this text is to provide practice and techniques for successful expository writing experiences.

Beginners cannot expect to be proficient with expository writing. Knowledge of capitalization, punctuation, spelling, basic grammar, and paragraph structure are some of the necessary prerequisite skills. Students who have developed good reading and study habits will be able to put their thoughts and ideas into writing more easily than those who consistently forget homework assignments and miss deadlines. Intermediate-level students are ready and able to use context clues, understand figures of speech, summarize, draw conclusions, and read critically. A well prepared 10-year-old can become a competent writer of expository compositions.

The lessons in this book contain introductions, drills, and practices for crucial language objectives which are then applied to expository writing. First, the skills necessary to identify and distinguish between instructional and informative writing are introduced. This is followed by lessons that help young writers create quality paragraphs that focus on a topic, clearly address the purpose, and have ample supporting details and a logical organization. Next, techniques to incorporate descriptive language that clarifies and enhances ideas are explained. Character sketches, interviews, personal narratives, and friendly letters are spiced up with nifty nouns, vivid verbs, and other colorful figures of speech. The last section contains methods and strategies to employ while gathering information for research topics. Reference skills, skimming and scanning techniques, and outlining plans are presented and applied to longer reports. Students are instructed to use the four-step writing process (i.e., prewriting, writing, revising, publishing) to develop *contrast*, *explanatory*, *cause and effect*, and other expository essays. All writing is evaluated using the four-point rubric scale.

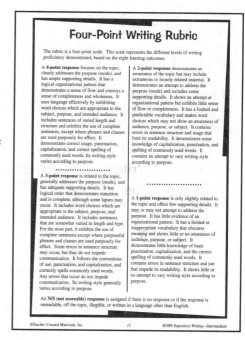

The use of technology and audiovisual materials is also included. Each lesson has a computer-connection component. Teachers are encouraged to have their students use word-processing programs, to explore the World Wide Web, and to incorporate the latest software as young writers compose their papers. Many of the publishing projects offer unique ideas for sharing and displaying the students' work in front of an audience. These final, correct copies of their writings can also be collected into portfolios so that students can look back over their work and sometimes use an old composition as a starter for a new one.

This book contains many familiar ideas and concepts about expository writing. These lessons have been tried, tested, and modified with students and have yielded positive results. Writing is one of the most difficult tasks teachers demand their students to perform. The lessons and activities contained in this book will help your students face the challenge with enthusiasm and effectiveness.

Standards for Writing
Grades 3–5

Accompanying the major activities of this book will be references to the basic standards and benchmarks for writing that will be met by successful performance of the activities. Each specific standard and benchmark will be referred to by the appropriate letter and number from the following collection. For example, a basic standard and benchmark identified as **1A** would be as follows:

Standard 1: Demonstrates competence in the general skills and strategies of the writing process

Benchmark A: Prewriting: Uses prewriting strategies to plan written work (e.g., uses graphic organizers, story maps, and webs; groups related ideas; takes notes; brainstorms ideas)

A basic standard and benchmark identified as **4B** would be as follows:

Standard 4: Gathers and uses information for research purposes

Benchmark B: Uses encyclopedias to gather information for research topics

Clearly, some activities will address more than one standard. Moreover, since there is a rich supply of activities included in this book, some will overlap in the skills they address; and some, of course, will not address every single benchmark within a given standard. Therefore, when you see these standards referenced in the activities, refer to this section for complete descriptions.

Although virtually every state has published its own standards and every subject area maintains its own lists, there is surprising commonality among these various sources. For the purposes of this book, we have elected to use the collection of standards synthesized by John S. Kendall and Robert J. Marzano in their book *Content Knowledge: A Compendium of Standards and Benchmarks for K–12 Education* (Second Edition, 1997) as illustrative of what students at various grade levels should know and be able to do. The book is published jointly by McREL (Mid-continent Regional Educational Laboratory, Inc.) and ASCD (Association for Supervision and Curriculum Development). (Used by permission of McREL.)

Language Arts Standards

1. Demonstrates competence in the general skills and strategies of the writing process

2. Demonstrates competence in the stylistic and rhetorical aspects of writing

3. Uses grammatical and mechanical conventions in written compositions

4. Gathers and uses information for research purposes

Standards for Writing
Grades 3–5 *(cont.)*

Level II (Grades 3–5)

---

1. Demonstrates competence in the general skills and strategies of the writing process

---

A. Prewriting: Uses prewriting strategies to plan written work (e.g., uses graphic organizers, story maps, and webs; groups related ideas; takes notes; brainstorms ideas)

B. Drafting and Revising: Uses strategies to draft and revise written work (e.g., elaborates on a central idea; writes with attention to voice, audience, word choice, tone, and imagery; uses paragraphs to develop separate ideas)

C. Editing and Publishing: Uses strategies to edit and publish written work (e.g., edits for grammar, punctuation, capitalization, and spelling at a developmentally-appropriate level; considers page format [paragraphs, margins, indentations, titles]; selects presentation format; incorporates photos, illustrations, charts, and graphs)

D. Evaluates own and others' writing (e.g., identifies the best features of a piece of writing, determines how own writing achieves its purposes, asks for feedback, responds to classmates' writing)

E. Writes stories or essays that show awareness of intended audience

F. Writes stories or essays that convey an intended purpose (e.g., to record ideas, to describe, to explain)

G. Writes expository compositions (e.g., identifies and stays on the topic; develops the topic with simple facts, details, examples, and explanations; excludes extraneous and inappropriate information)

H. Writes narrative accounts (e.g., engages the reader by establishing a context and otherwise creates an organizational structure that balances and unifies all narrative aspects of the story; uses sensory details and concrete language to develop plot and character; uses a range of strategies such as dialogue and tension or suspense)

I. Writes autobiographical compositions (e.g., provides a context within which the incident occurs, uses simple narrative strategies, provides some insight into why this incident is memorable)

Standards for Writing
Grades 3-5 *(cont.)*

J. Writes expressive compositions (e.g., expresses ideas, reflections, and observations; uses an individual, authentic voice; uses narrative strategies, relevant details, and ideas that enable the reader to imagine the world of the event or experience)

K. Writes in response to literature (e.g., advances judgements; supports judgements with references to the text, other works, other authors, nonprint media, and personal knowledge)

L. Writes personal letters (e.g., includes the date, address, greeting, and closing; addresses envelopes)

2. Demonstrates competence in the stylistic and rhetorical aspects of writing

A. Uses descriptive language that clarifies and enhances ideas (e.g., describes familiar people, places, or objects)

B. Uses paragraph form in writing (e.g., indents the first word of a paragraph, uses topic sentences, recognizes a paragraph as a group of sentences about one main idea, writes several related paragraphs)

C. Uses a variety of sentence structures

3. Uses grammatical and mechanical conventions in written compositons

A. Writes in cursive

B. Uses exclamatory and imperative sentences in written compositions

C. Uses pronouns in written compositions (e.g., substitutes pronouns for nouns)

D. Uses nouns in written compositions (e.g., uses plural and singular naming words; forms regular and irregular plurals of nouns; uses common and proper nouns; uses nouns as subjects)

E. Uses verbs in written compositions (e.g., uses a wide variety of action verbs, past and present verb tenses, simple tenses, forms of regular verbs, verbs agree with subjects)

F. Uses adjectives in written compositions (e.g., indefinite, numerical, predicate adjectives)

G. Uses adverbs in written compositions (e.g., to make comparisons)

H. Uses coordinating conjunctions in written compositions (e.g., links ideas using connecting words)

I. Uses negatives in written compositions (e.g., avoids double negatives)

Standards for Writing
Grades 3-5 *(cont.)*

J. Uses conventions of spelling in written compositions (e.g., spells high-frequency, commonly misspelled words from appropriate grade-level list; uses a dictionary and other resources to spell words; uses initial consonant substitution to spell related words; uses vowel combinations for correct spelling)

K. Uses conventions of capitalization in written compositions (e.g., titles of people; proper nouns [names of towns, cities, counties, and states; days of the week; months of the year; names of streets; names of countries; holidays]; first word of direct quotations; heading, salutation, and closing of a letter)

L. Uses conventions of punctuation in written compositions (e.g., uses periods after imperative sentences and in initials, abbreviations, and titles before names; uses commas in dates and addresses and after greetings and closings in a letter; uses apostrophes in contractions and possessive nouns; uses quotation marks around titles and with direct quotations; uses a colon between hours and minutes)

---

4. Gathers and uses information for research purposes

A. Uses a variety of strategies to identify topics to investigate (e.g., brainstorms, lists questions, uses idea webs)

B. Uses encyclopedias to gather information for research topics

C. Uses dictionaries to gather information for research topics

D. Uses key words, indexes, cross-references, and letters on volumes to find information for research topics

E. Uses multiple representations of information (e.g., maps, charts, photos) to find information for research topics

F. Uses graphic organizers (e.g., notes, charts, graphs) to gather and record information for research topics

G. Compiles information into written reports or summaries

The Expository-Writing Rubric

Accountability—Expectations—Assessment

A **rubric** is an assessment tool which is particularly useful in scoring students' written responses. Often assignments or test questions require short answers and extended responses that are subjective and complex. In order to justify an assessment or grade, teachers need a device that describes levels of acceptable performance. A rubric presents teachers and students with expectations that clearly show how a composition will be evaluated. A rubric allows assessment to be objective and consistent.

Once students become familiar with the purpose and application of a rubric, they can work with teachers to create rubrics for future lessons and assignments. Goals, expectations, and focuses will become clearer as the young writers become part of the process of assessment. Involving students in the making of rubrics helps them take more responsibility for their own learning. When exact information about scoring and instructional objectives is communicated, pupils are more active and willing to engage in realistic problem solving. In order to accurately evaluate student achievement in these complex and vague behaviors, work with the class to explain, develop, and apply a rubric.

Rubrics for expository writing are four-point scales that represent the different levels of writing proficiency demonstrated, based on the identified learning outcomes.

A **distinguished**, or **four-point**, response significantly increases an audience's understanding and knowledge of the topic. The paper's purpose and subject are clearly defined; pertinent examples, facts, and statistics are noted; and conclusions or ideas are supported by data or evidence. The paper is well organized, proofread, and the main points are summarized in the composition's closing statements. A child who receives a four-point score is advanced beyond the proficiency standards and can independently write expository paragraphs.

A **proficient**, or **three-point**, response raises an audience's understanding and awareness of most of the topic's main points. It is successful in defining the paper's purpose and subject. Some examples, facts, and statistics are noted, and conclusions or ideas are supported by adequate references to data or evidence. The topic may need to be narrowed or researched further. Capitalization, punctuation, grammar, and spelling errors are few and do not confuse the reader. A child who receives a three-point score meets the established proficiency standards and can usually write expository paragraphs.

An **apprentice**, or **two-point**, response raises an audience's understanding and knowledge of some of the topic's points. An attempt is made to define the paper's purpose and subject, but the organization needs improvement. The main ideas are too broad, insufficiently researched, and haphazardly presented. More supporting samples, facts, and statistics are necessary in order for the composition to clearly communicate its intended message. Poor proofreading and careless mistakes are common. A child receiving this score is below the established proficiency standards and requires assistance when writing expository paragraphs.

A **novice**, or **one-point**, response does not increase an audience's knowledge or understanding of the topic. A weak attempt is made to define the paper's purpose and subject, while examples, facts, and statistics are noticeably missing. Readers are confused by sentence fragments, incomplete paragraphs, and by the lack of supporting data and evidence. There appears to be no attempt to revise or proofread, and legibility is poor. A child receiving this score is well below the established proficiency standards and is in need of intervention when writing expository paragraphs.

Four-Point Writing Rubric

The rubric is a four-point scale. This scale represents the different levels of writing proficiency demonstrated, based on the eight learning outcomes.

A **4-point response** focuses on the topic, clearly addresses the purpose (mode), and has ample supporting details. It has a logical organizational pattern that demonstrates a sense of flow and conveys a sense of completeness and wholeness. It uses language effectively by exhibiting word choices which are appropriate to the subject, purpose, and intended audience. It includes sentences of varied length and structure and exhibits the use of complete sentences, except where phrases and clauses are used purposely for effect. It demonstrates correct usage, punctuation, capitalization, and correct spelling of commonly used words. Its writing style varies according to purpose.

• • • • • • • • • • • • • • • • • • •

A **3-point response** is related to the topic, generally addresses the purpose (mode), and has adequate supporting details. It has logical order that demonstrates transition and is complete, although some lapses may occur. It includes word choices which are appropriate to the subject, purpose, and intended audience. It includes sentences that are somewhat varied in length and type. For the most part, it exhibits the use of complete sentences except where purposeful phrases and clauses are used purposely for effect. Some errors in sentence structure may occur, but they do not impede communication. It follows the conventions of use, punctuation, and capitalization, and correctly spells commonly used words. Any errors that occur do not impede communication. Its writing style generally varies according to purpose.

A **2-point response** demonstrates an awareness of the topic but may include extraneous or loosely related material. It demonstrates an attempt to address the purpose (mode) and includes some supporting details. It shows an attempt at organizational pattern but exhibits little sense of flow or completeness. It has a limited and predictable vocabulary and makes word choices which may not show an awareness of audience, purpose, or subject. It contains errors in sentence structure and usage that limit its readability. It demonstrates some knowledge of capitalization, punctuation, and spelling of commonly used words. It contains an attempt to vary writing style according to purpose.

• • • • • • • • • • • • • • • • • • • •

A **1-point response** is only slightly related to the topic and offers few supporting details. It may or may not attempt to address the purpose. It has little evidence of an organizational pattern. It has a limited or inappropriate vocabulary that obscures meaning and shows little or no awareness of audience, purpose, or subject. It demonstrates little knowledge of basic punctuation, capitalization, and the correct spelling of commonly used words. It contains errors in sentence structure and use that impede its readability. It shows little or no attempt to vary writing style according to purpose.

An **N/S (not scoreable) response** is assigned if there is no response or if the response is unreadable, off the topic, illegible, or written in a language other than English.

Create Your Own Rubric

How Do I Begin?

First of all, it is important to know that your prompt or task and your rubric are part of the same package. Secondly, it is vital to realize that this is an interactive procedure—you will write, try out, and revise your prompt/rubric package until it tells you what you really want to know. Getting it exactly right the first time is a result of years of experience or plain luck!

Write the Rubric First

It is probably easier to write the rubric first. A three-point rubric is the easiest, and you can begin at any point. The three points of a three-point rubric parallel one another and reflect different levels of the same skills. The "High Pass" contains all of the features of the "Pass," either in identical form or as a more advanced variation. "Needs Revision" considers parallel features, but they may be expressed as negatives.

Decide what you will be assessing in your rubric. Once you have decided what to include in your rubric, all criteria must appear in some form in all of the points.

Write the Prompt

Your prompt should be written to elicit a response that will allow assessment of the points in your rubric. If your "High Pass" requires the students to write more than one complete sentence, you should not instruct them to write "a sentence." This seems really obvious, but sometimes you will not catch this kind of thing until you are reading a batch of papers. If you suddenly realize that you are not getting any "High Pass" papers, you may want to look back at the wording of your prompt.

Revise, Revise, Revise

There are many reasons to consider revising your rubric and/or prompt. Look for some of these:

1. No high papers
   —Did I require something I have not taught?
   —Did I require something in the rubric which was not in the prompt?
2. All high papers
   —Did I want this result? (It is possible for everyone to do really well.)
3. No passing papers
   —Were the directions wrong or easy to misinterpret?
   —Was the format different from our usual assignments?
4. Results inconsistent with the way I see my class
   —Do I need to look at the prompt/rubric package?
   —Do I need to take another look at the class?

Rubrics Are Power

Feeling comfortable with rubric writing gives you a powerful position in the assessment process. You will nearly always be able to justify your results and demonstrate how you obtained them.

Create Your Own Rubric *(cont.)*

Use this blank form to create your own scoring rubric for a writing sample.

Scoring Rubric

Score 4: High Pass

Student

-
-
-

Score 3: Pass

Student

-
-
-

Score 2: Needs Revision

Student

-
-
-

Score 1: Does Not Pass

The Basics of Punctuation

Clear, concise writing of any kind relies on a number of factors, including interesting word choices, solid sentence construction, and adherence to the topic being addressed. One major area which cannot be overlooked is the proper use of punctuation. The punctuation marks—and their uses—which are most commonly used and needed at this level are listed below:

The Basics of Punctuation

Apostrophes

❑ **Use apostrophes for contractions**.
  You've got to come and visit soon. I'm missing you!

❑ **Use apostrophes to show possession or ownership with nouns**.
  Amber's dad found David's wallet in the Fletchers' car.

❑ **Use apostrophes in the place of omitted numbers in dates**.
  John's dad thinks that the best cars were made in the '50s.

  The U.S. hockey team took home the gold medal in the '80 Olympics.

Colons

❑ **Use a colon right after the greeting in a business letter.**
  Dear Sirs: Dear Mrs. Gonzales:

❑ **Use a colon to introduce a list.**
  Please bring the following items to school: white paper, colored pencils, and a compass.

❑ **Use a colon between the hour and the minutes of the time of day.**
  5:30 A.M.   3:15 P.M.

❑ **Use a colon to introduce a long direct quotation**.
  At the Galaxy Alien Convention, the keynote speaker said:

> *Things are looking up for space aliens these days. We can now make Earthlings better looking! Our handsome bug eyes, snake-like tongues, and slimy ears are easily cloned to replace ugly human features. Not only can we help the poor things raise their self-esteem, but we will finally be able to view them without throwing up!*

(**Hint:** There are no quotation marks around the passage above. That is because they are not used with a long direct quote. Instead, indent both sides of the quote to set it off from the other text).

The Basics of Punctuation *(cont.)*

Commas

❏ **Use a comma between two independent clauses joined by *or*, *and*, or *but*.**

There are always creative excuses for not turning in homework, but no excuse is acceptable.

My dad loves music, and my mom loves to sing.

❏ **Use a comma after a dependent clause that comes at the beginning of a sentence.**

Even though I forgot my notes, I still did a good job on my speech.

❏ **Use a comma between words, phrases, or clauses that are a series of three or more things.**

I will be writing a report that is brilliant, insightful, and a delight to read.

My mother asked me to feed the dog, take out the trash, and fold all my clothes.

My brothers are Jason, Michael, and Chris.

❏ **Use commas to set apart hundreds, thousands, and millions, etc., when writing numbers.**

My brother had 234,556,000 telephone messages when we got home, and they were all from girls!

❏ **Use a comma to set apart the city from a state and a street from a city.**

When I grow up I intend to live at 12234 Monster Mash Lane, Transylvania, PA.

❏ **Use a comma after the day and after the year in a date that appears in the middle of a sentence.**

President Kennedy was shot on November 22, 1963, in Texas.

❏ **Use a comma after a greeting and a closing in a letter to a friend or relative.**

Dear Granny,

Lovingly yours,

❏ **Use a comma after introductory words at the beginning of a sentence or after an interjection (an introductory exclamation).**

Yes, of course you may dye your hair purple.

No kidding, I dyed my hair purple.

❏ **Use a comma after an interjection that is not an exclamation.**

Oh, I don't know what I'll do.

❏ **Use a comma to separate the person to whom you are speaking from the rest of the sentence.**

Julie, I heard you dyed your hair purple.

❏ **Use a comma to set off dialogue.**

Her mom asked, "What on earth happened to your hair?"

She said, "You don't remember?" and she walked into the light so her mom could get a better look. "You told me it was okay to dye it purple."

❏ **Use commas to set off interruptions.**

My dog will do the craziest things. The other day, for example, he was eating broccoli.

The Basics of Punctuation *(cont.)*

Commas *(cont.)*

❏ **Use commas to set off appositives (words or phrases that explain, identify, or rename a noun or pronoun).**
Licorice, my dog, tore a hole in the screen to get a tortilla!

My sister, the world's smartest girl, forgot her orthodontist appointment.

❏ **Use commas to set off phrases.**
Positive-negative film, rarely used except in the movie industry and by some photographers, will take negatives, prints, and slides.

A drooling, snarling dog chased me across the park, over a fence, and into a trash bin.

❏ **Use commas between two like adjectives that modify the same noun.**
We drove all day across the dry, dusty desert.

Dashes

❏ **Use a dash to indicate a sudden break in a sentence.**
There is one thing that really bugs me about my brother—no, actually there are a zillion things—but it bugs me most when my friends call and he puts them on hold and forgets all about them.

❏ **Use a dash to add emphasis to a word, a series of words, a phrase, or a clause.**
Let me just remind you that you will need to complete all the requirements—have a title page, a bibliography, and a video—in order to get the highest possible grade.

❏ **Use a dash to show that someone's speech is being interrupted.**
Hello—yes, I remembered—what?—oh, okay—no, that really won't be necessary—no, really—I mean it—no, of course not—really, you don't need to—I really mean it, you don't need to—don't.

Ellipses

❏ **An ellipsis is three spaced periods used to replace words that have been left out or to indicate a pause in dialogue.**
Ah . . . well . . . it's like this . . . ah . . . aliens came down . . . that's it . . . they came down in this huge saucer and sucked up my homework with some strange, vacuum-like device!

Twinkle, twinkle . . . like a diamond in the sky.

❏ **When an ellipsis ends a sentence, add a period, making a total of four dots.**
I was thinking of going with you, but. . . .

Exclamation Points

❏ **An exclamation mark is used to show strong feeling after a word, a phrase, or an exclamatory sentence. (Be careful with exclamation points; they should not be overused. And don't ever use multiple exclamation marks all in a row!!!)**
Oh, no! My underwear just fell out the window!

The Basics of Punctuation *(cont.)*

Hyphens

❑ **Use a hyphen with two-part numbers.**
forty-eight   twenty-three

❑ **Use hyphens when writing fractions as words.**
one-fourth   four-tenths

❑ **Use hyphens to create new words.**
You've got an I-know-something-you-don't-know look on your face.

❑ **Use hyphens for compound nouns and adjectives.**
drive-through bank   four-year-old boy

G-rated   e-mail

Parentheses

❑ **Use parentheses around words or phrases that add information or make an idea more clear.**
For more information about llama toenails, read chapter 13 (pages 56–72).

The national park had something for everyone, including the fit (trails, mountain climbing, and whitewater rafting), the consumer (shops and concession stands), the curious (nature centers, museums, and ranger tours), and the tired (hammocks, benches, and cabins).

He asked his neighbor Paul (who's a whiz with cars) to help him repair his truck.

❑ **Use parentheses around an abbreviation after you have written the full name.**
My high school is on the same street as Jet Propulsion Lab (JPL).

Periods

❑ **Use a period at the end of a declarative or imperative sentence that is not an exclamation.**
Always turn off the light when you leave the room.

My puppy chewed on my algebra book.

In the future, most of us will be telecommuting.

❑ **Use periods after initials.**
A. A. Milne   Mr. P. J. Winterhouse

❑ **Use periods after abbreviations. (Postal abbreviations for states are an exception.)**
P.O. Box 987
234 Slippery Hill St.
Mt. Awesome, CA

Question Marks

❑ **Use a question mark at the end of an interrogative sentence (a question) and to show doubt about the accuracy of a figure or fact.**
What were you thinking when you decided to do that?

By the year 2040 (?), marine biologists will be living in laboratories on the ocean floor.

The Basics of Punctuation *(cont.)*

Quotation Marks

❑ **Use quotation marks to set off the words of a direct quote.**

When my brother woke up this morning, he came out of his room all rumpled and said, "I don't know what President Lincoln would do because I haven't asked him."

❑ **Use quotation marks to indicate the title of an article in a magazine or newspaper.**

I cut out an article titled "My Best Friend, Llama" from yesterday's paper.

❑ **Use quotation marks to indicate the title of a chapter.**

Read the chapter titled "My Brother, the Denizen of the Deep."

❑ **Use quotation marks to indicate the titles of essays and short stories.**

My essay, "How I Almost Spent My Summer Vacation," was in the school newspaper.

My mom just sold a short story titled "Jackie, the Mad Hugger."

❑ **Use quotation marks to indicate the titles of songs and poems.**

My dad keeps listening to "Free as a Bird" on the CD player.

I am going to read "Bed in Summer" by Robert Louis Stevenson.

❑ **Use quotation marks around certain words used in a special way.**

I can't believe I got "punctuation" right on the spelling test!

Please send me your e-mail address, or I will have to send this by "snail mail."

I called my brother a "dork" after he called me a "dweeb."

❑ **A quote within a quote uses only one quotation mark at each end of the inside quote.**

She said, "He told me that 'The Little Princess' is his favorite poem."

"Listen," Amber said, "Mr. Zone clearly stated, 'Do not leave CDs in the CD-ROM drive!'"

Semicolons

❑ **Use a semicolon to join the independent clauses of a compound sentence when you are not using a comma and a conjunction.**

My mom got a scanner for the computer; I couldn't wait to try it.

❑ **Use a semicolon in front of a conjunction when you are joining two simple sentences.**

She usually adores frozen yogurt; however, today she didn't want any.

❑ **Use a semicolon in a series of three or more items when commas are used within those items.**

Our talent show will include Jazz, a group of dancers; Klutzy Kyle, a magical extravaganza; Barknikov, a poodle ballet dancer; and Spring Showers, a folk singer.

Editing Marks

Throughout this text, the process of proofreading is suggested as a vital step in the writing process. To be sure that all students use the same "language" when editing their papers and their peers' papers, the following list of marks has been provided:

Proofreading Marks

Editor's Mark	Meaning	Example
ℓ	Delete	It was was very tiny.
≡	Capitalize	the boy ran quickly.
/	Use lowercase	Many Athletes ran in the marathon.
∧	Add a word	I want an ice cream sundae.
RO	Run-on sentence	Who's there what do you want?
frag.	Sentence fragment	Although the peddler's cart. frag.
SP	Spelling error	Monkies swung in the trees.
∽	Reverse letters or words	Five books on were the shelf.
⊙	Add a period	Children played all day⊙
∧	Add a comma	I like apples peaches, and pears.
∨	Add an apostrophe	John's puppy is cute.
⌄ ⌄	Add quotation marks	Help! I cried.
¶	Begin a new paragraph	"Hello," said Carla. "Hi," Beth replied.
#	Make a space	I love Frenchfries.
⌒	Close the space	He lives in the country side.
stet	Do not delete (Let it stand.)	The beautiful swan flew away.

The
Components
of
Expository
Writing

What Is Expository Writing?

Intermediate students will be required to read, write, and interpret expository text. At this age level, the basic skills taught and practiced during the elementary years start being applied to problem solving, descriptive writing, and other tasks that demand higher-level thinking. This lesson is designed to teach students to recognize expository writing and to identify whether an author is trying to describe a process or retelling the details of a significant event.

Goal:

The students will be able to distinguish expository writing from narrative writing.

Objectives:

1. Given main idea sentences, students will classify them as fiction or nonfiction.

2. Given expository paragraphs, students will classify them as either instructional or informative.

Materials:

- Worksheet #1 (page 24)

- Worksheet #2 (page 25)

- Worksheet #3 (page 26)

Procedure:

I. Lesson Introduction

A. Begin this lesson on identifying expository writing with an anecdote about pets. Discuss the best pets to own and the lessons one can learn from taking care of these creatures. Bring up the topic of exotic pets and ask the students to relate a story about someone they know who owns an unusual bird, reptile, or primate. Finally, ask them to list stories they have read and heard about imaginary pets and exotic animals. Inform the pupils that factual stories that describe animals or tell about the care and training of animals are called nonfiction. Authors use expository writing techniques to instruct and inform. Myths, legends, fables, and other made-up stories are fiction. Authors use narrative writing techniques to tell these tales.

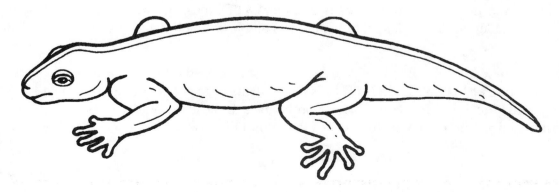

What Is Expository Writing? *(cont.)*

B. After you have identified and defined nonfiction and fiction, compare and contrast the characteristics of each. Nonfiction is instructional or informative. Science and social studies are the classes that rely upon nonfiction books, periodicals, and other factual sources. Language arts classes use the prose and poetry of many authors to help make the study of language interesting and entertaining. Read the following titles aloud and have students classify them as either nonfiction or fiction:

1. *World Book Encyclopedia* (nonfiction)

2. *To Kill a Mockingbird* (fiction)

3. *Information Please Almanac* (nonfiction)

4. *Rand McNally Atlas of the United States* (nonfiction)

5. *Betty Crocker Cookbook* (nonfiction)

6. *Tuck Everlasting* (fiction)

7. *The Biography of Abraham Lincoln* (nonfiction)

8. *The Wish Giver* (fiction)

9. *The Phantom Tollbooth* (fiction)

10. *The Lion, the Witch, and the Wardrobe* (fiction)

The students must be able to distinguish between nonfiction and fiction in order to identify and write expository paragraphs. Exercise A on the lesson worksheet and the reinforcement/reteaching worksheet will help you evaluate the students' mastery of this concept.

II. Lesson Body

A. Expository is the most common form of writing and reading assigned in school. Science projects, research papers for history, and mathematical word problems are a few examples. Proficiency tests contain extended response writing that may require a student to write summaries, journal entries, directions, memos, or informational articles. Expository writing is nonfiction that explains and describes a process or presents facts, details, and background information about past events and discoveries.

B. Instruct the students to read the paragraph on Worksheet #1. Have them classify it as nonfiction or fiction. Next, have them discuss where this article may have come from and where a person might find further information on its topic. Examine the second paragraph and identify what process is being explained. Finally, locate the opinion statement in the last paragraph and listen to any student reaction. Explain that this is an example of expository writing. Its purpose is to inform the reader about the demand for rare pets and how this is causing a crisis for endangered species.

C. Distribute Worksheet #2. Exercise A asks the students to read a main idea sentence, then classify it as nonfiction or fiction. Exercise B asks the students to read two paragraphs, then label them as either instructional or informative. These problems and those on Worksheet #3 will allow students to drill, practice, and review the objectives taught in this lesson.

What Is Expository Writing? *(cont.)*

III. Lesson Conclusion

A. Conclude the lesson by having the students state or write the definitions of the following terms: *nonfiction, fiction, instructional paragraph*, and *informative paragraph*. Students also need to create a list of five examples of expository writing and where it can be found and applied. At this point, pupils are able to distinguish between expository writing and narrative writing.

B. Writing Applications:

1. **Instructional:** Assign the students to write a paragraph that explains how to give a pet a bath. The topic sentence will tell what the paragraph intends to explain. Supporting sentences list any materials that will be needed and the step-by-step instructions. Have the students read each other's writing and test the processes for proper sequence and clear wording.

2. **Informative:** Instruct the students to write a report that tells how the name for a family pet was chosen. The writing must describe the animal and how it was acquired. Other supporting sentences should detail the naming process the family went through and how they finally settled on a name.

C. Publishing:

1. The papers and pictures of the pets can be displayed on a bulletin board. Cover up the names of the writers so those reading the compositions will have to guess to whom each pet belongs.

2. Have the students use a word-processing program to reproduce their final drafts. Instruct them to print all instructional paragraphs in one font (e.g., Arial) and all informative paragraphs in another font (e.g., Courier).

IV. Evaluation

A. Lesson Objectives: Use the discussion questions, Worksheet #2, and Worksheet #3 to measure student progress and mastery of the objectives.

B. Writing Applications: Use the four-point rubric scale on page 11 to determine if students *can independently, can usually,* or *require assistance to* write expository paragraphs.

What Is Expository Writing?
Worksheet #1

Expository writing instructs or informs its reader.

Read the following informative paragraph. On the blank lines below, describe how the paragraph informs the reader.

Endangered Animals/Endangered Pets

How many of your friends have unusual pets? Most of us know someone who owns a dog that can do tricks or a cat with a unique personality. More people, though, are collecting and keeping rare animals in their homes. It is common to find primates, reptiles, and exotic birds being traded and sold in the United States, Europe, and Japan.

The problem is that many of these chimpanzees, iguanas, and scarlet macaws have been hunted or trapped illegally. First, a poacher steals a newborn from its nest. Then, a dealer buys it for a few dollars. Next, a smuggler sneaks the animal across the border. The creature is then offered to any number of buyers and traders. The rarer the species, the bigger the profit for dealers.

It is against the law to poach, smuggle, and sell endangered animals. Criminals have preyed upon poor, uneducated people who do this for them. Dealers will pay only a small amount to a villager or young child to steal baby monkeys, snakes, and parrots. The next step is to find another person to risk taking these creatures through international airports and customs. This illegal animal trade has become a multi-billion dollar business.

Not every marmoset, tortoise, or cockatoo you see has been stolen from its home in the wild. A majority of rare animals have been purchased legally, and most pet stores refuse to deal in stolen pets. Countries in Africa, Asia, and South America have toughened their poaching laws and have increased their border wildlife inspections.

Orangutans, pythons, and toucans survive best in the wild. It is against the natural order to swipe a precious creature from its home and display it in a cage just for the entertainment of human beings.

_____

_____

_____

_____

What Is Expository Writing?
Worksheet #2

Fiction is a story from someone's imagination. **Nonfiction** is a story that is true.

Exercise A

Read each sentence and decide if it would be found in a fictional story or in nonfiction. Write your answer on the line.

example: Charles Lindbergh was the first to fly solo across the Atlantic Ocean. *nonfiction*

1. Columbus is the capital city of Ohio. _____

2. The Nile River is the longest river in Africa. _____

3. It was a very stormy night when the aliens landed. _____

4. Detroit is the home of Ford Motor Company. _____

5. A genie granted the slave girl three wishes. _____

6. Space Rangers from planet Zoar came to the rescue. _____

7. Your heart beats about 76 times a minute. _____

8. Noisy squirrels threw a party in the forest glade. _____

9. Our babysitter seemed unaware of the mutant zombies outside. _____

10. Latitude lines measure from north to south. _____

Exercise B

Read each paragraph below and decide if it is **instructional** (describes a process) or **informative** (reports the details of a significant event). Circle the correct answer.

> This is how to make a toasted cheese sandwich. You need two slices of bread, cheese, butter, a knife, a stove, and a frying pan. First, butter one side of each piece of bread. Next, place one piece, buttered side down, in the frying pan. Then put one or two slices of cheese on that piece of bread. After that, place the other piece of bread on top, buttered side up. Finally, turn on the stove and toast each side for two or three minutes. Now you are ready to eat this tasty luncheon treat.
>
> **Instructional**   or   **Informative**

> Florence Griffith-Joyner was once the fastest woman in the world. Her record times in the 100-meter dash and 200-meter dash still stand today. During the 1988 Summer Olympics, her speed, strength, and style helped her win three gold medals. Nicknamed "Flo-Jo," she was known for her beautiful long hair and brightly colored fingernails. After she retired from competition, Florence Griffith-Joyner wrote children's books, designed uniforms for professional athletes, and served on the President's Council on Physical Fitness and Sports. "Flo-Jo" will be remembered as a remarkable athlete and as a productive private citizen.
>
> **Instructional**   or   **Informative**

What Is Expository Writing?
Worksheet #3

Fiction is a story from someone's imagination. **Nonfiction** is a story that is true.

Exercise A

Read each sentence and decide if it belongs in a fiction or nonfiction book. Explain your answer.

Examples: Pete the Porcupine yelled, "Danger!" when he heard the hunters approach.
This sentence belongs in a fiction book because animals cannot talk.

All animals need oxygen to live.
This belongs in a nonfiction book because it is informative.

1. Lief Erikson settled a colony in North America long before the English, French, and Spanish.

   _____

   _____

2. Auto racing is a popular sport in many countries around the world.

   _____

   _____

3. An evil witch cast her doomsday spell over the sleeping village.

   _____

   _____

4. Aliens took over the local radio station and broadcasted their invasion plans.

   _____

   _____

5. Add one gallon of water to every 50 pounds of concrete mix.

   _____

   _____

6. The prince and the mermaid lived happily ever after in a kingdom under the sea.

   _____

   _____

7. On January 25, 1998, John Elway led the Denver Broncos to a victory in Super Bowl XXXII.

   _____

   _____

What Is Expository Writing?
Worksheet #3 *(cont.)*

Exercise B

On the lines below, rewrite this paragraph in its correct sequence. Then tell if the paragraph is **informative** or **instructional.**

1. Return to your classroom when the all-clear signal is given.

2. Do not talk as you file out of the building.

3. When the fire bell sounds, stop what you are doing.

4. Walk to the designated safe area in the schoolyard.

5. Line up quietly, and wait for further instructions.

_____

_____

_____

_____

_____

_____

_____

_____

_____

_____

_____

> This paragraph is   **informative**   or   **instructional**.

Standards and Benchmarks: 1A, 1B, 1C, 1L, 2A, 2B, 2C, 3A, 3B, 3C, 3D, 3E 3F, 3G, 3H, 3I, 3J, 3K, 3L

The Writing Process

Successful writers utilize a basic four-step system to create, develop, and present their thoughts and ideas. *Prewriting*, *writing*, *revision*, and *publishing* are the components of the writing process. Intermediate students learn to distinguish between stories and reports and do their first serious independent research. This lesson is designed to introduce the writing process to this age level and apply its objectives to future lessons and assignments.

Goal:

Students will apply the steps of the writing process to expository writing.

Objectives:

1. Students will identify and define the terms: *prewriting*, *writing*, *revision*, and *publishing*.

2. Students will create a thank-you note utilizing the four steps of the writing process.

Materials:

- Worksheet #1 (page 31)
- Worksheet #2 (page 32)

Procedure:

I. Lesson Introduction

A. Begin the lesson with an anecdote about the best present you ever received. Allow time for some of the students to share their similar experiences. Discuss how one would show appreciation towards the gift giver, both in person and in writing. Review the concept of a "thank-you note," and tell the students they will be using the four steps of the writing process to create one.

B. Introduce the four steps of the writing process.

1. *Prewriting*: gathering materials and writing ideas

2. *Writing*: putting your thoughts in writing for the first time

3. *Revising*: adding to and deleting from your writing and then applying proofreading skills

4. *Publishing*: making a written piece into a final product

The Writing Process *(cont.)*

II. Lesson Body

A. The first step in the writing process is *prewriting*. Explain to the students that in this step, a writer identifies and narrows the topic upon which to write. The audience is identified, and information is gathered and organized. Interviews, research, and personal experience are the most common starting points for expository writing. Some other strategies include the following:

   1. Prereading: Reading books and periodicals that feature information about your topic.

   2. Questionnaires and Surveys: Prepare a question-and-answer sheet to give to those you cannot interview face to face.

   3. Cause and Effect: Study how one event brings about or influences another.

   Once a writer has found the one idea, it is wise to organize the facts and figures with a word cluster or outline.

B. The second step in the writing process is putting thoughts down on paper for the first time. Examine notes, outlines, and any other graphic organizer employed and begin to communicate the message in complete sentences. One thought should flow into the next. Grammar, capitalization, punctuation, spelling, and legibility will be scrutinized and corrected later. Most writing teachers label this step "the rough draft."

C. *Revision* follows all writing. Here is where a writer makes changes to improve the writing. Reread and check to make sure the paper's message is clear and stays on the given topic. An author will delete material that deviates from the topic and possibly do more background research. It is strongly suggested that another adult or peer help the writer with editing and proofreading. This is the final check before a writer shows off his or her work in public.

D. *Publishing* is sharing the work with others. It can be as simple as making a legible copy to turn in to a teacher or as complicated as having it printed in a literary magazine. This is the author's chance to produce an attractive copy of the work then compare and contrast it with the writings of others. It is suggested that teachers and students keep a portfolio of most of their written compositions.

E. Writing Process Lesson Worksheet (page 31)

   1. Students will first match the definition with the step of the writing process.

   2. Students will read a writing sample and label it as either prewriting, writing, revising, or publishing.

   3. The teacher may use this as a guided lesson for those who are struggling or as independent work for those who are on their way to mastery of this concept.

The Writing Process *(cont.)*

III. Lesson Conclusion

A. Conclude the lesson by having the pupils define the steps of the writing process in their own terms. Next, cite examples of expository writing and how to apply the four steps of the writing process.

   1. Informative Writing: Character Sketch

      a. prewriting: researching and interviewing

      b. writing: organizing the information into paragraphs

      c. revising: checking sentences for sequence and proofreading

      d. publishing: displaying the character sketch on a bulletin board and directing others to read it

   2. Instructional Writing: Making a Paper Airplane

      a. Prewriting: gathering and organizing the materials needed to make the project

      b. Writing: creating the step-by-step instructions using the signal words *first*, *next*, *after that*, and *finally*

      c. Revising: proofreading and testing the instructions with a volunteer

      d. Publishing: reading the paragraph to a large group and having them follow along while building paper airplanes

B. Reinforcement and Reteaching

   1. Use the reinforcement/reteaching worksheet for those who are struggling or need the necessary review.

   2. Students will list the four steps of the writing process in their correct sequence, define them, and then write a thank-you note to a person they admire.

C. Writing Applications: Instruct the students to write a thank-you note to a friend or relative. The pupils are not limited to writing about gifts but may write about acts of kindness or other favors directed towards them.

D. Publishing

   1. Encourage the students to apply the four steps of the writing process to organize, write, and share their final notes.

   2. Computer Connection: For Exercise B of the reinforcement worksheet, schedule time for the students to search the Internet for information about the celebrity to whom they are writing. Scan for a Web page and current address to which to send their thank-you notes. They also may find an e-mail address to keep on file for future correspondence.

IV. Evaluation

A. Use the lesson practice exercises, lesson worksheet, and the reinforcement/reteaching worksheet to measure student progress and mastery of the objectives.

B. Writing Applications: Use the four-point rubric scale to determine if students *can independently, can usually,* or *require assistance t*o write expository paragraphs.

The Writing Process
Worksheet #1

*Writers use a **four-step process** to narrow topics, write, revise, and share their ideas.*

Exercise A

Match the definition on the left with the correct term on the right.

1. _____ Sharing the final composition with others
2. _____ The way a writer discovers and develops an idea
3. _____ Editing, proofreading, and making changes
4. _____ Putting ideas down on paper for the first time

A. Prewriting
B. Writing
C. Revising
D. Publishing

Exercise B

Read each sentence and decide if it is an example of *prewriting, writing, revising,* or *publishing.* Write your answer on the line.

1. Narrow a broad topic to a more exact person, place, thing or idea.

   _____

2. Submit a written piece to a student newspaper or literary magazine.

   _____

3. Check capitalization, punctuation, spelling, and handwriting for errors.

   _____

4. Use notes to remember facts and details.

   _____

5. Supply the audience with a legible copy of the composition.

   _____

6. Create a questionnaire or survey to discover likes and interests.

   _____

7. Refer to an outline to place the main idea and supporting sentences in proper sequence.

   _____

8. Check the first sentence to see if it captures a reader's attention.

   _____

The Writing Process
Worksheet #2

*Writers use a **four-step process** to narrow topics, write, revise, and share their ideas.*

Exercise A

List the four steps of the writing process, and then write a definition for each.

1. _____

   _____

2. _____

   _____

3. _____

   _____

4. _____

   _____

Exercise B

Write a thank-you note to a celebrity you admire. The message should state how the person has inspired, helped, or set a good example for you and your friends. Use the four steps below and the frame on the following page to compose your letter.

Prewriting:
1. Who are you writing to?
2. What has this person done for you?

Writing:
1. Thank-you notes are short letters of appreciation for a gift or favor.
2. Be sure you follow the format of a friendly letter:
   a. Heading
   b. Greeting
   c. Body
   d. Closing

Revising:
1. Did you state the purpose of the note in the first sentence?
2. Did you keep the message friendly and brief?
3. Did you follow the format of a friendly letter?
4. Did you proofread for correct capitalization, punctuation, spelling, and legibility?

Publishing:
1. Rewrite the first draft in your best handwriting.
2. People tend to read and treasure neat and well-written notes and cards more than sloppily made ones.
3. Send the thank-you note to the person.

Thank-You Note Frame

Paragraph Perfection

At the intermediate level, students will be required to respond to essay questions and writing prompts in paragraph form. It is essential that pupils learn the elements of a well-written paragraph and practice creating them. This lesson is designed to assist students in putting sentences together in order to write quality paragraphs.

Goal:

Students will write expository paragraphs that contain a main idea, supporting sentences, and a conclusion.

Objectives:

1. Given a group of sentences, the students will eliminate those that do not relate to the main idea.

2. Given a group of sentences, the students will identify the main idea and then rewrite them in paragraph form.

Materials:

- Worksheet #1
- Worksheet #2

Procedure:

I. Lesson Introduction

A. Begin the lesson with a discussion about complete sets. Collectibles in complete sets are more valuable than partial sets. Having a complete set of tools enables one to get a job done efficiently. Matching dishes, coordinated furniture, and common decorations are more appealing than a hodgepodge arrangement. Stress that a paragraph is a complete set of sentences about one idea. A set of paragraphs will make up a report with a beginning, middle, and ending.

B. Make the analogy between a paragraph and a chair. A good paragraph is like a sturdy chair. The seat cushion and back represent the main idea. The four legs are the supporting sentences while the floor underneath is the conclusion. A two-legged paragraph just will not stand up. Three supports are adequate, but four are best. Chairs with five or more legs become too complex and even comical. Reinforce the idea that a well-written paragraph will have about six sentences—a main idea sentence, four supporting sentences, and a conclusion.

Paragraph Perfection *(cont.)*

C. A reinforcement/reteaching worksheet is also included as part of the lesson. The above exercises are repeated with different topics. An added paragraph asks the students to identify its components and to edit out any unnecessary information. After completing the tasks on these two worksheets, students will have created and practiced writing quality paragraphs while being exposed to informative and instructional expository writing.

II. Lesson Body

A. Introduce the lesson worksheet. In the first exercises, students will be given sentences that form an expository paragraph and others that do not belong. Students are to locate and eliminate the sentences that do not support the given main idea. Reinforce the concept of paragraph writing by instructing the learners to rewrite all the related sentences in the form of a paragraph.

B. The second exercise does require the pupils to rewrite the given sentences as a paragraph. First, the students must organize and place the sentences in proper sequence. Start by identifying the topic sentence; next, logically order the supporting sentences; and finish with the concluding sentence.

III. Lesson Conclusion:

A. Close the lesson by having the pupils identify the elements of a quality paragraph. Restate the paragraph/chair analogy. Remind the students that information and instruction are best communicated through well-written paragraphs. Supporting sentences contain details about the main idea, and unrelated facts must be located and removed during revision. Finish the thought with a concluding sentence that restates the main idea. The paragraph is complete when the writer has a set of sentences about one main idea.

B. Writing Applications: Instruct the students to write a paragraph about a collection each has. The composition will describe what it is that they collect, how many items are in the collection, and its monetary and personal value. Students are to add details that explain how this collection was started and what the future plans are for it.

C. Publishing Project

   1. Secure a building showcase and have the students bring in their collections for display. The descriptive paragraphs can be laminated and included as part of this informative presentation.

   2. Computer Connection: Direct the students to go online and check out some of the auction Web sites. Have them search for similar items that are in their collections and discover the current bids and asking prices.

IV. Evaluation

A. Lesson Objectives: Use the discussion questions and worksheets to measure student progress and mastery of the objectives.

B. Writing Applications: Use the four-point rubric scale to determine if students *can independently, can usually,* or *require assistance to* write detailed descriptions of familiar, persons, places, objects, or experiences.

Paragraph Perfection
Worksheet #1

*A **well-written paragraph** has a topic sentence, approximately four supporting sentences, and a conclusion.*

Exercise A

Decide which of these sentences belong in a paragraph about hurricanes. For each sentence, answer **Yes** or **No**.

_____ 1. Hurricanes are dangerous tropical storms.

_____ 2. They form over the warm waters of an ocean.

_____ 3. It rained all night on Saturday and Sunday.

_____ 4. Violent winds spin counterclockwise around the center, or eye.

_____ 5. Warm water and hot air make hurricanes stronger.

_____ 6. Tornadoes are dangerous, spinning funnel clouds.

_____ 7. Florida has a coast on the Atlantic Ocean.

_____ 8. When wind speeds reach 74 miles per hour, the storm becomes a hurricane.

_____ 9. Once these tropical storms hit land, they begin to weaken.

Exercise B

For the sentences below, organize them and rewrite them in paragraph form. Underline the main idea sentence once and the conclusion twice. Remember to indent the first sentence.

1. Gutters overflowed, and streets became raging rivers.

2. Everything became eerie, quiet, and calm.

3. The sky darkened with ominous storm clouds.

4. After 20 minutes, the sun came out and a rainbow appeared overhead.

5. All of a sudden, rain poured down in sheets.

6. A tremendous thundercrack sent us to the basement, seeking shelter.

_____

_____

_____

_____

_____

_____

_____

_____

Paragraph Perfection
Worksheet #2

A ***well-written paragraph*** has a topic sentence, approximately four supporting sentences, and a conclusion.

Exercise A

Write **Yes** if a sentence below tells about the following main idea and **No** if it does not: *Ohio was a home to seven American presidents.*

_____1. Ulysses S. Grant grew up on an Ohio farm.

_____2. Cincinnati was the home of Rutherford B. Hayes.

_____3. Benjamin Harrison had a beard.

_____4. James A. Garfield lived in Orange, Hiram, and Mentor, Ohio.

_____5. President McKinley was assassinated in 1901.

_____6. Many were born in log cabins or small cottages.

Exercise B

Write the following sentences as a paragraph. Write the main idea sentence first. Next, write the supporting sentences in an order that makes sense. Remember to indent the first sentence.

1. Trees cannot grow on ruins before they were built.

2. Every year a tree will grow a new ring of wood.

3. Archaeologists use trees to help them figure out how old a place is.

4. By counting tree rings, we can tell that a ruin is at least as old as the trees that grow there.

5. Scientists count the number of rings in tree trunks to discover the ages of trees.

_____

_____

_____

_____

_____

_____

_____

_____

_____

_____

Paragraph Perfection
Worksheet #2 *(cont.)*

Exercise C

On the lines below, rewrite the following paragraph. Underline the sentence that states the main idea. Cross out the sentence that does not belong.

There are many things to do at a county fair. You can sample some of the foods local farmers grow. Rabbits, guinea pigs, hamsters, and other small animals will be on display. There will be demonstrations of horsemanship and sheep shearing to watch. At night, entertainers will sing and dance. The Ferris wheel is my favorite ride. A county fair is an exciting place to visit.

_____

_____

_____

_____

_____

_____

_____

_____

_____

_____

_____

_____

_____

_____

_____

Terrific Topic Sentences

A *topic sentence* states a paragraph's main idea. It also serves to capture the reader's attention. Most expository paragraphs begin with declarative sentences, but a writer can add variety by starting with a question, command, or interjection that expresses strong feelings or emotions. This lesson is designed to give students practice in writing topic sentences that make main ideas clear and also appealing to their audience.

Goal:

Students will write paragraphs with topic sentences that capture their reader's attention.

Objectives:

1. Given a writing prompt, the students will create a topic sentence.

2. Given a topic sentence, the students will restate it as a question, command, or exclamation.

Materials:

- Worksheet #1 (page 42)
- Worksheet #2 (page 43)

- newspapers and other periodicals

Procedure:

I. Lesson Introduction

A. Begin the lesson with a discussion about whales. Talk about their size, where whales live, and how these creatures interact with humans. Ask volunteers to create a declarative sentence, interrogative sentence, imperative sentence, and an exclamatory sentence using the topic "killer whales" (orcas). Explain to the pupils that a topic sentence needs to be interesting and attention-getting. Most expository writing begins with topic sentences that are declarative, or statements. Sometimes a writer will add variety to a piece by beginning with a question, command, or interjection that expresses emotion.

B. Direct the learners to read the paragraph about whales that goes with this lesson. Have them locate and state the topic sentence. Next, the pupils will brainstorm and attempt to restate that sentence in the form of a question, command, or exclamation. A group of sample responses is provided.

Terrific Topic Sentences *(cont.)*

II. Lesson Body

A. Introduce the lesson practice worksheet. The students will be given writing prompts and then asked to create a list of topic sentences. Declarative statements will be acceptable for these exercises. When these statements are given, the writers are asked to transform each into a question, command, or exclamation.

B. A review of the four types of sentences (declarative, interrogative, imperative, and exclamatory) and end punctuation may be necessary (page 41). Remind the students that most expository writing begins with declarative sentences, but writers will occasionally vary their styles and use questions, commands, and exclamations to maintain interest and challenge their audiences.

C. For reinforcement and reteaching, first gather together a collection of newspapers and periodicals. Have the pupils identify a story of interest and then state its topic sentence. After that, practice transforming these into questions, commands, and exclamations.

D. Extend the lesson by using these articles to practice summary writing skills. Also practice writing conclusion sentences in the form of questions, commands, or exclamations. This will provide a unique way to end compositions.

III. Lesson Conclusion

A. Close the lesson by having the pupils restate the purpose of a topic sentence. They must also list different strategies that can be applied to make topic sentences more interesting and attractive to their audience. Students will be asked to employ these techniques in future writing assignments.

B. Writing Applications: Whales like the orca, dolphin, and porpoise are often trained to entertain or assist humans with certain water-related tasks. Instruct the students to write a paragraph about an animal that performs in a show or is trained to work with people for a common goal. It may be an animal with which they have had personal experience or one observed at a circus, water park, or on television. Tell them to begin by stating topic sentences in the form of questions, commands, or exclamations.

C. Publishing Project:

1. Group students together that have written about the same or similar animals. Have them read their compositions to each other and then share their reactions and feelings within the small group.

2. Computer Connection: Many animal theme parks, zoos, and circuses have home pages listed on the Internet. Allow the pupils to locate and view a few of these Web sites to help them research further information for their writing applications.

IV. Evaluation:

A. Use the discussion questions and worksheets to measure student progress and skill mastery.

B. Writing Applications: Use the four-point rubric scale to determine if students *can independently, can usually,* or *require assistance to* write detailed descriptions of familiar, persons, places, objects, or experiences.

The Four Types of Sentences

Declarative Sentence

An insect is sometimes called a bug.

Interrogative Sentence

Do you know anything about insects?

Imperative Sentence

Close the lid to the bug box.

Exclamatory Sentence

Oh no, the bugs are escaping!

End Punctuation

Type of Sentence	Punctuation Mark
Declarative Sentence	.
Interrogative Sentence	?
Imperative Sentence	.
Exclamatory Sentence	!

Terrific Topic Sentences
Worksheet #1

*A **topic sentence** states the main idea and must capture a reader's interest.*

Of the 78 species of whale, the orca (or killer whale) is the most feared. These mammals live in families called pods and swim in all the oceans of the world. One is most likely to find them in the colder waters of the Arctic and Antarctic regions of Earth. A tall dorsal fin and a black and white body make them easily recognizable. Their rounded snouts and bullet-shaped bodies allow orcas to swim at speeds up to 40 miles per hour. A killer whale is the only whale that eats warm-blooded prey. Often it takes 300 pounds of fish, squid, and other marine animals a day to satisfy this beast's huge appetite. The orca may appear to be friendly or playful at water parks or on television, but this wild animal is one of the most ferocious in nature.

1. What is the topic sentence of the paragraph about? _____

   _____

2. Use the information in the paragraph above to write the following:

   a. an interrogative sentence

      Example: What do you know about killer whales?

      _____

      _____

   b. an imperative sentence

      Example: Read these facts about orcas.

      _____

      _____

   c. an exclamatory sentence

      Example: Orcas are fascinating beasts!

      _____

      _____

Terrific Topic Sentences
Worksheet #2

A *topic sentence* states the main idea and must capture a reader's interest.

Exercise A

Read the following list of writing ideas. Create a topic sentence for each.

1. the best place to go swimming _____

   _____

2. my favorite amusement park ride _____

   _____

3. going fishing with a friend _____

   _____

4. enjoyable board games to play _____

   _____

5. our family's most valuable possession _____

   _____

6. a day at the races _____

   _____

7. staying overnight at grandmother's house _____

   _____

8. the surprise party _____

   _____

9. when the wheels came off _____

   _____

10. the broken eyeglasses _____

    _____

Exercise B

Read the following topic sentences. Rewrite each in the form of a question, command, or exclamation.

1. Our vacation on a tropical island was very exciting. _____

   _____

2. I made too many mistakes the first day of school. _____

   _____

3. A police car pulled into our driveway. _____

   _____

4. My parents brought home twins from the hospital. _____

   _____

5. It was past midnight when I heard something coming up the stairs. ____

   _____

Superb Summaries

The most common type of expository writing assigned in class and asked for on proficiency tests is the summary. Students will communicate their knowledge of character, setting, and plot and demonstrate their understanding of theme, purpose, and point of view. A quality summary can be written in one or two paragraphs. This lesson is designed to help students apply the skills taught and practiced in this section on summary writing.

Goal:

Students will write a one-paragraph summary about a current event.

Objectives:

1. Given a sample summary, the students will identify its main idea, supporting sentences, and conclusion.

2. Given a main idea sentence, students will restate it (paraphrase) using their own words.

3. After reading an expository essay, the students will summarize its topic and main ideas.

Materials:

- Worksheet #1 (page 47)
- Worksheet #2 (page 48)
- newspapers and periodicals

Procedure:

I. Lesson Introduction

A. Begin with a short, personal narrative about flying. Summarize an experience you have had with planes, hot-air balloons, or helicopters. Ask the students to share any similar stories from their lives. Remind each speaker to describe only the important events. Too many details will confuse an audience or make them lose interest.

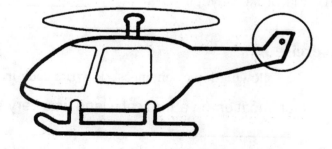

B. Introduce the "Guidelines for Writing a Summary." Read and review each guideline, and point out examples from the students' oral summaries that reflected these guidelines. Explain that teachers ask pupils to summarize in order to find out to what degree lessons, readings, and presentations have been understood.

Superb Summaries *(cont.)*

II. Lesson Body

A. Distribute Worksheet #1. Instruct the students to read it carefully and to note the composition's main idea. Demonstrate how elements of the practice summary relate to the given guidelines. Have the pupils complete Exercise B. Conclude by discussing where the original article that was summarized came from.

B. Paraphrasing Practice: Copying anything from the original material is not summarizing. A writer must express an article's main idea and important details in his or her own words. The worksheet for paraphrasing offers the students an opportunity to practice this skill.

III. Lesson Conclusion:

A. First, restate that summary writing is a method to discover if a student has understood what has been read, heard, or viewed. Summarizing is a common task required by intermediate teachers. Most standardized tests ask students to write summaries about a story or concept. Review and read aloud the six guidelines for summary writing.

B. Writing Applications: Arrange for the class to view a news program targeted at young people. *NickNews*, *Discovery News*, and *Newsdepth* are some popular examples. List and discuss the featured stories on the telecast. Identify and write the main ideas and important details. Have the students choose a story and write a summary. Instruct them to conclude the paragraphs with statements of their opinion.

C. Publishing:

1. Post the summaries on a current events bulletin board, and invite others to read them. Include space for readers to make comments. Disagreements are acceptable if they are expressed in an appropriate manner.

2. As a culminating activity, students can apply their expository writing skills to the creation of a newscast. Choose two pupils to serve as news anchors. Their job will be to introduce each story and to organize them into a program. Group the remaining students into threes or fours. The small groups will write short skits based on ideas borrowed from current events. One group member will be the reporter, and the others will role-play being witnesses, victims, and perpetrators. Videotape the skits as if they were a local news report.

3. Computer Connection: Most local, national, and international newspapers and news services have up-to-date current-events Web sites. Allow the pupils to locate and read a few selections from these sources. They will find further information on their topic and also discover other people's points of view.

IV. Evaluation

A. Use the lesson discussion questions, practice exercises, and paraphrasing worksheet to measure student progress and mastery.

B. Writing Applications: Use the four-point rubric scale to determine if each student *can independently, can usually,* or *requires assistance to* write expository paragraphs.

Guidelines for Writing a Summary

❏ Review the material and take note of the topic, main ideas, and important details.

❏ Identify the topic in the first sentence.

❏ Use your own words (paraphrase) to state the main ideas in a logical order.

❏ Conclude by restating the topic. You may express your opinion in the concluding sentence.

❏ Summaries are limited to a paragraph or two.

❏ Copying anything from the original material is not a summary.

Superb Summaries
Worksheet #1

*A **summary** of a story reports the main idea and most important details.*

Exercise A

Read this summary. Cross out the sentence that does not belong.

On March 21, 1999, Bertrand Piccard and Brian Jones became the first humans to complete a nonstop trip around the world in a balloon. People often take rides in hot-air balloons at carnivals. They flew 29,056 miles in 20 days. Their quest began in Switzerland, then took them eastward. The balloon, *Breitling Orbiter 3*, traveled over Asia, the Pacific Ocean, North America, and the Atlantic Ocean. This 180-foot tall, helium-filled craft moved along at speeds up to 130 miles an hour, while 43,000 feet in the air. After overcoming several critical mission problems, the pilots reached their goal and landed in an Egyptian desert. Skill, state-of-the-art equipment, and good luck were all necessary for Piccard and Jones to make aviation history in a balloon.

Exercise B

Review the paragraph above and the Guidelines for Writing a Summary (page 46). Complete the following.

1. Underline the summary's main idea sentence once and its conclusion sentence twice.

2. Write your opinion about the historic journey of Piccard and Jones.

_____

_____

_____

_____

3. Rewrite the following sentence, using your own words: *After overcoming several critical mission problems, the pilots reached their goal and landed in an Egyptian desert.*

_____

_____

_____

Superb Summaries
Worksheet #2

Paraphrasing is taking the ideas you have read and expressing them in your own words.

Exercise A

Rewrite each sentence, using your own words.

Example: The history of balloon flight dates back over 200 years.

Over 200 years ago, people first traveled in balloons.

1. The first passengers in a hot-air balloon were a sheep, a duck, and a rooster.

_____

_____

2. In 1785, humans successfully crossed the English Channel riding in a balloon.

_____

_____

3. Experiments with hot-air balloons did not start in North America until 1793.

_____

_____

4. One hundred seventy-five years passed before people made it across the Atlantic Ocean in a balloon.

_____

_____

5. Pilots Bertrand Piccard and Brian Jones recently completed the first nonstop trek around the world in a balloon.

_____

_____

Superb Summaries
Worksheet #2 *(cont.)*

Exercise B

On the lines below, use the sentences you wrote in Exercise A to create a summary paragraph. First, add a topic sentence that introduces the topic. Then, recopy your answers from sentences 1–5. Finally, add a concluding sentence that restates the topic and includes your opinion about it.

_____

_____

_____

_____

_____

_____

_____

_____

_____

_____

_____

_____

_____

_____

_____

_____

_____

_____

_____

_____

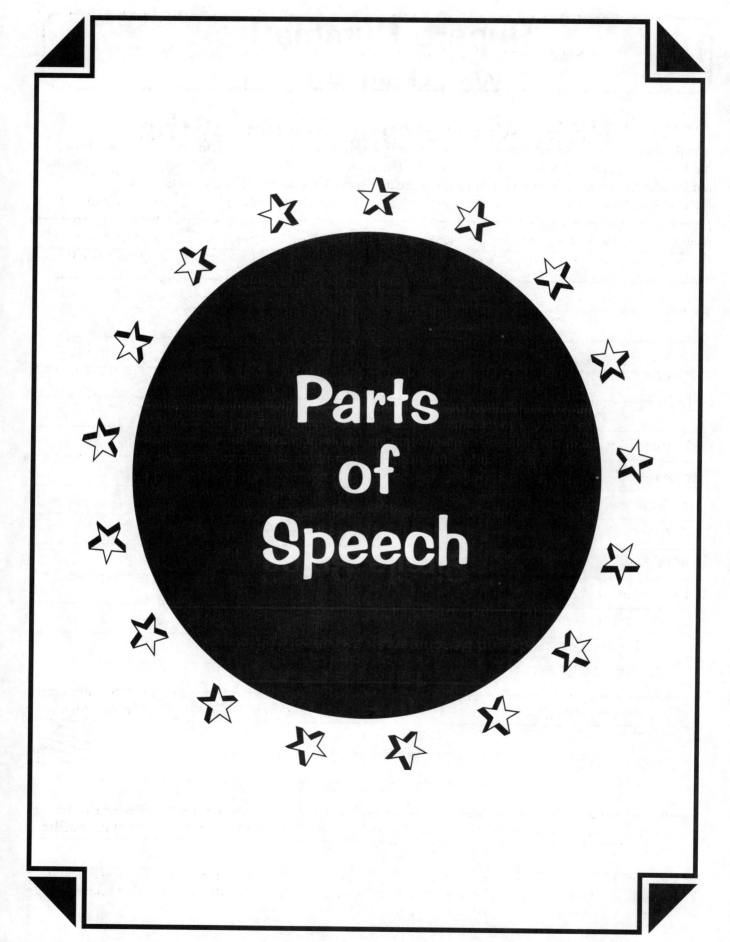

Parts
of
Speech

50
©Teacher Created Materials, Inc.

Nifty Nouns and Vivid Verbs

Nouns identify who or what a composition is about. *Verbs* supply action and feeling. At the intermediate level, *dog*, *car*, and *town* become *Labrador*, *sedan*, and *metropolis*. Likewise, a sixth grader no longer *drinks* milk but instead *gulps*, *guzzles*, or *takes a swig*. This is the age where young writers must proofread for nondescript or vague details and actions. It is the time to advance beyond the basics and make paragraphs stay on the topic and be interesting. This lesson is designed to help students use more descriptive language when writing expository papers.

Goal:

Students will use exact nouns and verbs to add details to their writing.

Objectives:

1. Given a sentence containing vague nouns or verbs, students will replace them with more descriptive synonyms.

2. Students will write and revise compositions using clear and precise nouns and verbs.

Materials:

- Worksheet #1 (page 53)
- Worksheet #2 (page 54)
- 3" x 5" index cards (3)

Procedure:

I. Lesson Introduction

A. Write the following sentences on the chalkboard.

   1. I gave my mother *a flower.*

   2. The soccer game will start in *awhile.*

   Point out the vague or nondescript nouns. Have student volunteers replace those words with more exact nouns. Then, say the new sentences aloud. State that exact or specific nouns clarify main ideas and make sentences more interesting.

B. Write one of these words on each of three 3" x 5" index cards:

   1. yell   2. jump   3. think

   Ask for volunteers to pantomime each word, and have the others make several guesses. List the student responses—right or wrong—on the chalkboard. Explain that like nouns, exact or specific verbs also make an idea clear and informative.

C. Review the thesaurus. Remind the learners that this reference source is a book of synonyms and antonyms. Use it to locate descriptive nouns, verbs, adjectives, and adverbs. Replace common, overused words with those found in a thesaurus.

Nifty Nouns and Vivid Verbs *(cont.)*

II. Lesson Body

A. Worksheet #1 offers practice with identifying and replacing vague and overused words for people, places, and things. At first, clues are given and pupils fill in the blanks. In the second exercise, pupils' answers will vary. Encourage the students to refer to a thesaurus and make their modified sentences unique.

B. Worksheet #2 offers similar practice with overused actions and state-of-being words. Once again, make a thesaurus available for those who need creative assistance. As an added challenge (for both nouns and verbs), instruct the pupils to rewrite their answers from the second exercise as a paragraph. Add a concluding sentence to the other five, and each will have created informative and instructional examples of expository writing.

III. Lesson Conclusion

A. Ask the students to state in their own words why it is important to identify and replace vague, overused nouns and verbs.

1. Say the word "clothes" and have volunteers list more exact examples and synonyms.

2. State the following sentence. "A sports car went down the street." Ask for volunteers to repeat the statement with more descriptive verbs and their synonyms.

3. Direct their attention to the thesaurus. Review its basic elements and purpose.

B. Writing Applications

1. Assign a character sketch. Tell the students to describe a friend's looks, characteristics, and interests. The topic sentence should identify the person's most unique quality and the supporting sentences must be organized so the reader can visualize the subject. Reveal the person's identity only in the concluding sentence. Revise with an emphasis on replacing vague or overused nouns with more exact synonyms.

2. Instruct the learners to think of an adventure or a good time they have had with the person who was the subject of their character sketch. Tell them to write the story of this event. Have them use transition words—*first, next, then, after that, finally,* etc.—to help organize it. Revise with an emphasis on replacing common verbs with vivid, more descriptive synonyms.

C. Publishing

1. Have the students create collages that relate to their narrative paragraphs. Paste the final copies of their paragraphs in the centers of the collages and display them on a bulletin board.

2. Computer Connection: Direct the students to use a word-processing program to produce a final copies of their character sketches. Assemble them into a classroom "Who's Who." Assign a small group of students to organize the compositions into one volume and then design a cover and table of contents to make it complete.

IV. Evaluation

A. Use the discussion questions, practice exercises, and lesson worksheets to measure student progress and mastery.

B. Writing Applications: Use the four-point rubric to determine if the student *can independently, can usually,* or *needs assistance to* use descriptive details to enhance and clarify ideas.

Nifty Nouns
Worksheet

Exact nouns add details and make the writing more interesting.

Exercise A

The first sentence contains a vague noun in italics. The second sentence contains a blank or blanks for an exact noun that can replace the vague noun. Fill in the blanks to complete the sentences.

Example: A *sound* came from Kelly's room.

A *scream* came from Kelly's room.

1. Dad worked at his desk for a *time.*

   Dad worked at his desk for a(n) _____.

2. The *story* was enjoyable.

   The _____ was enjoyable.

3. We visited that historic *place.*

   We visited that historic _____.

4. My brother put *pieces* together.

   My brother put _____ and _____ together.

5. I added *stuff* to the recipe.

   I added _____, _____, and _____ to the recipe.

Exercise B

Circle the vague nouns in these sentences. Replace them with more exact nouns and rewrite each sentence. Refer to a thesaurus for more descriptive words.

1. My relative has a coin collection.

   _____

2. He owns many types made of different metals.

   _____

3. Most are from this country, but some are from other countries.

   _____

4. A few have images of people, and a few have images of animals.

   _____

5. This relative keeps them in a place in his house.

   _____

Challenge: On a separate sheet of paper, rewrite the sentences created for Exercise B in paragraph form. Add a concluding sentence to make it complete.

Vivid Verbs
Worksheet

Exact verbs supply a reader with more information and make writing more interesting.

Exercise A

The first sentence contains a vague verb in italics. The second sentence contains a blank for an exact verb that can replace the vague verb. Fill in the blanks to complete the sentences.

Example: Uncle Wally *laughed* at the joke.
　　　Uncle Wally *snickered* at the joke.

1. I *ran* to catch the early bus.

   I _____ to catch the early bus.

2. Claire *likes* pizza with extra cheese.

   Claire _____ pizza with extra cheese.

3. That pitcher can *throw* a wicked fast ball.

   That pitcher can _____ a wicked fast ball.

4. Our teacher had to *say* the directions three times.

   Our teacher had to _____ the directions three times.

5. Big Jake *ate* five potato pancakes.

   Big Jake _____ five potato pancakes.

Exercise B

Circle the vague verbs in these sentences. Replace them with more exact verbs and rewrite each sentence. Refer to a thesaurus for more descriptive words.

1. It is exciting to go in an airplane.

   _____

2. First, you sit and put on a seat belt.

   _____

3. Next, the engines start.

   _____

4. Then, the plane rolls down the runway.

   _____

5. Suddenly, you are in the air.

   _____

Challenge: On a separate sheet of paper, rewrite the sentences created for Exercise B in paragraph form. Add a concluding sentence to make it complete.

Adjective Attention

Intermediate writers must be able to advance beyond sentences composed of simple subjects and simple predicates. At this age, students' compositions begin to have more details and less repetition. Nouns and verbs give life to stories or reports, but it is the adjectives and adverbs that make paragraphs rich and colorful. Adjectives add shape, size, sound, smell, and taste. This lesson is designed to help students use adjectives to make their writing paint a word picture.

Goal:

Students will use a variety of adjectives to make their expository writing more descriptive.

Objectives:

1. Given an adjective, students will classify it as "how many" or "what kind."

2. Students will identify adjectives when they occur in context.

Materials:

- Adjective Attention worksheet (page 57)

Procedure:

I. Lesson Introduction

A. Write the word *bird* on the chalkboard and have the students brainstorm a list of descriptive words that answer the following questions:

   1. What do birds look like?

   2. What do birds sound like?

   3. What do birds feel like?

   4. How do birds (chicken, cornish hen, etc.) taste?

   5. How many birds are there? (Use numbers and non-numeral words such as *few*, *a lot*, *several*, *bunches*, *zillions*, etc.)

Say that an adjective is a part of speech that describes a noun or pronoun. Adjectives answer the questions *what kind* or *how many*.

B. Write the following sentence on the chalkboard: "Set those _____ birds free." Call on volunteers to fill in the blank with a word that answers the question *what kind* or *how many* and to say the complete sentence. After giving several examples, inform the pupils that authors use adjectives to make their writing descriptive and more exact.

Adjective Attention *(cont.)*

II. Lesson Body

A. The first task on the adjective worksheet will help the students practice and review classifying this part of speech. A list of words is presented and students must decide if each tells *what kind* or *how many*. Expand the exercise by having the students brainstorm sentences (oral or written) with words from this section.

B. After the pupils have practiced classifying adjectives, the next task is to identify this part of speech in context. At first the adjectives are highlighted, and then the clues are discontinued. Finally, the learners are asked to supply adjectives to complete sentences of their own creation.

III. Lesson Conclusion

A. Ask the students to define an adjective in their own words. Have them classify five examples of words that tell *what kind* or *how many*. Restate that authors use a variety of adjectives to make their work more descriptive and exact. A well-written paper uses adjectives to create a word picture in the imagination of the reader.

B. Writing Application: View a program about tropical birds or take a field trip to a local aviary. Instruct the children to select a specific bird and write about it. Stress the use of adjectives to describe the bird's color, shape, size, and sounds.

C. Publishing:

  1. Have the pupils read their bird reports to the class without revealing the birds' identities. Together, list and organize the given details and try to guess the type of bird.

  2. Computer Connection: Encourage the students to use a word-processing program when they rewrite their bird reports. Have them locate and highlight the adjectives as they occur in the composition.

IV. Evaluation

A. Use the lesson discussion questions, practice exercises, and adjective worksheet to measure student progress and mastery.

B. Writing Application: Use the four-point rubric scale to determine if students *can independently, can usually,* or *require assistance to* use descriptive language that clarifies and enhances ideas.

Adjective Attention
Worksheet

*An **adjective** describes a noun or pronoun. Adjectives usually answer the question* what kind *or* how many.

Exercise A

Decide if the adjectives answer the question *what kind* or *how many*. Write your answer on the line.

1. all _____
2. best _____
3. few _____
4. new _____
5. warm _____
6. blue _____
7. fast _____
8. long _____

9. seven _____
10. white _____
11. a lot _____
12. eight _____
13. funny _____
14. million _____
15. round _____
16. several _____

Exercise B

Tell if the bold-faced adjectives answer the question *what kind* or *how many*.

1. There were **six** birds in our tree. _____
2. **Small** sparrows are **good** singers. _____
3. Blue jays eat **lots** of acorns and nuts. _____
4. An **old** crow sat on a **dead** branch. _____

Read each sentence. **Circle** all the adjectives that answer the question *what kind* or *how many*.

5. People, young and old, enjoy watching birds.
6. The only equipment you need is a pair of eyes.
7. Good ears and a guide book are helpful, too.
8. Experienced bird watchers use powerful binoculars.

Read each sentence. **Underline** adjectives that tell *what kind* **once** and adjectives that tell *how many* **twice**.

9. Find a quiet spot in a wooded area.
10. After several minutes curious birds will visit you.
11. You should keep a record of the different birds in a small notebook.
12. These creatures play an important part in nature.

Challenging: Write six sentences describing a wild or pet bird. Use at least one adjective that tells what kind or how many in each sentence.

Appealing Adverbs

Adverbs can be difficult to master. Not only can this part of speech modify verbs, it also works with adjectives and other adverbs to make a composition more descriptive. Repeated practice is required not only at the intermediate level but also during the middle-grade and high-school years. This lesson is designed to help students practice identifying adverbs and using them to clarify and enhance ideas in expository writing.

Goal:

The students will use a variety of adverbs to make their expository writing more descriptive.

Objectives:

1. Given a familiar word, the students will create an adverb by adding the suffix /ly/.

2. Students will identify and classify adverbs when they occur in context.

Materials:

- Appealing Adverbs worksheet (page 60)

Procedure:

I. Lesson Introduction

Start the lesson with a discussion concerning fire and safety rules. Introduce the categories: *how, when, where,* and *to what extent.* Present the following situations and have the pupils brainstorm words that answer the question word categories.

1. exiting the classroom during a fire drill (*how, when, where,* and *to what extent*)

2. an ambulance rushing to an accident scene. (*how, when, where,* and *to what extent*)

3. cooking food on the stove (*how, when, where,* and *to what extent*)

4. building and extinguishing a campfire (*how, when, where,* and *to what extent*)

5. helping a friend who is injured (*how, when, where,* and *to what extent*)

State that an adverb is a part of speech that modifies verbs, adjectives, and other adverbs. Adverbs answer the question words *how, when, where,* and *to what extent.*

Appealing Adverbs *(cont.)*

II. Lesson Body

A. Distribute the Appealing Adverbs worksheet. These exercises offer many opportunities to create, locate, and write with adverbs. First, the pupils are presented a list of common words that can be transformed into adverbs by simply adding the suffix */ly/*. Extend this practice by asking volunteers to use each newly made adverb correctly in a sentence. Next, the learner is asked to identify an adverb and then classify it as *how, when, where,* and *to what extent*. Students are also to note the adverb location which will help them understand exactly what word in the sentence is being modified.

B. For an extra challenge, a list of six commonly heard adverbs are supplied, and the pupils must write them correctly in sentences of their own creation. What makes this task difficult is that the list presented contains adverbs that modify adjectives and other adverbs. It will be necessary to plan carefully and revise initial ideas in order to be successful with this exercise.

III. Lesson Conclusion

A. Ask the students to define an adverb in their own words. Have them list several examples in each category (*how, when, where,* and *to what extent*). Restate that authors use adverbs to clarify and enhance ideas. A well-written paper has a variety of adverbs.

B. Writing Applications: Arrange for a guest speaker from the local fire department or law enforcement agency to address the class. Before the visit, the students are to prepare interview questions to ask the firefighter or police officer. Tell the pupils to avoid questions that have "yes" or "no" answers; instead, they should try to use a few adverbs to make the inquiries clear and to the point. Students are to keep notes and write a summary of this experience.

C. Publishing

   1. Keep a classroom chart of adjectives and adverbs used and heard that are related to fire and safety issues. Listen for these parts of speech during the talk by the guest speaker. Also, examine the student-written summaries and any rules or posters located throughout the school building for examples to add to the chart.

   2. Computer Connection: Many companies that sell and service fire and safety equipment have online catalogs. Instruct the pupils to locate information and prices on firefighting and law enforcement items and then present either an oral or written report on their searches and findings.

IV. Evaluation

A. Use the discussion questions, practice exercises, and worksheet to measure student progress and mastery.

B. Writing Applications: Use the four-point rubric scale to determine if students *can independently, can usually,* or *require assistance to* use descriptive language that clarifies and enhances ideas.

Appealing Adverbs
Worksheet

*An **adverb** is a part of speech that describes a verb, adjective, or another adverb. Adverbs answer the questions how, when, where, or to what extent.*

Exercise A

Say each word to yourself. **Add** the suffix /ly/ to create adverbs. **Write** the **adverb** on the line provided.

1. bright _____
2. careful _____
3. helpless _____
4. rough _____
5. quick _____
6. curious _____
7. final _____
8. poor _____
9. quiet _____
10. soft _____
11. courageous _____
12. harmful _____
13. occasional _____
14. selective _____
15. successful _____

Exercise B

The **verb** is **underlined** in each sentence. **Circle** the **adverb** that describes the verb.

1. The fire <u>burned</u> wildly.

2. An alarm <u>sounded</u> loudly.

3. A fire engine <u>arrived</u> quickly.

4. They <u>worked</u> hard and fought the blaze.

5. All the flames <u>were</u> completely <u>extinguished</u>.

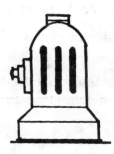

Appealing Adverbs (cont.)
Worksheet

Read each sentence. **Underline** the **adverbs** and then **write** the word it describes on the line.

6. Use matches carefully. _____

7. Old chemicals are often flammable. _____

8. Barbecue food items outdoors. _____

9. Handle fireworks responsibly. _____

10. Rapidly leave a dangerous area. _____

Read each sentence. **Underline** the adverbs. **Circle** the word(s) each describes.

11. Always follow the safety rules.

12. You never should hold fireworks.

13. Smoke is also deadly.

14. In an emergency, quickly dial 9-1-1.

15. Never play with fire.

Challenge: Adverbs can also modify an adjective or another adverb. Write six sentences that tell about an experience you have had with fire. Use one of the following adverbs in each sentence. Underline the word it describes.

always	quite	very
extremely	really	too

Figurative
Language

©Teacher Created Materials, Inc.

Simile Spice

A *simile* is a figure of speech that describes people, places, things, or ideas by comparing them to something else. The goal is to get a reader to look at something in a new, unique way. The basic terms that signal that a simile is being used are *like* and *as*. For advanced writers, *than* and *resembles* are key words that indicate an author is employing a simile. It is important to recognize and apply similes because this figure of speech adds to description and makes a composition more interesting to read. The purpose of this lesson is to have the students practice identifying and creating similes. After that, the students will include an example of this figure of speech in their expository writing.

Goal:

The students will use similes to clarify and enhance their expository writings.

Objectives:

1. Given a list of similes, students will read and discuss their meanings and then use them to create original examples.

2. Students will write a narrative paragraph that includes a simile.

Materials:

- Simile Spice worksheet (page 65)

Procedure:

I. Lesson Introduction

A. Introduce similes. Inform the students that authors use figures of speech to add details to their writing and to make the text more interesting. A simile compares two different people, places, things, or ideas. The simile phrase contains the signal words *like* or *as*. These words get a reader to look at and consider something from a different point of view.

B. Write the following examples on the chalkboard. Ask the students to identify what is being compared. Have them identify the signal words and describe how the phrase clarifies or enhances the main idea.

   1. The problems were like ants at a picnic.

   2. Denise was as angry as a bear in a trap.

C. Distribute the Simile Spice worksheet. Two more samples of simile are given, and these can be used to reinforce the lesson concept. Guide the pupils and have them share the similes they create for Exercise A. Exercise B helps the teacher confirm whether the students understand the meanings of similes in context.

Simile Spice *(cont.)*

II. Lesson Body

A. Writing Applications: Students are to each create a simile for their writing application. Students will compose a narrative paragraph about a family adventure or a favorite memory. The simile can occur anywhere in the story, but it might fit best in the first or last sentence.

B. Prewriting: Direct the pupils to look through a few family photo albums in order to identify a topic upon which to write. Tell them to search for memories of a special holiday, a humorous event, or a thrilling experience the family has shared.

    1. Have the students create a simile that best describes the story's main idea. Use it anywhere in the paragraph, but it may make for a good topic sentence or a fantastic final thought.

    2. Here are some sample topic sentences.

        a. "*I felt just like a king* during my surprise birthday party."

        b. "My *smile was as wide as a jack-o'-lantern's* when we arrived at Disney World."

C. Writing: Remind the students to include only the important details and omit those that have no bearing on the story. Unnecessary information will only confuse the reader. Review the time-order words (first, next, then, after that, last). This will help writers organize the events and assist readers in understanding the story's sequence.

D. Revising and Proofreading

    1. Instruct the students to read their narratives aloud to someone who is a good listener. Ask the audience if there were any details that were unclear or did not belong in the story. Also, have them check if the narrative told of only one incident and if time-order words were used to begin each sentence.

    2. The rough draft must be proofread for capitalization, punctuation, grammar, and spelling errors. Pupils are to add a title and rewrite legibly or use a word-processing program to create the final copy.

E. Publishing: Make a list of all the similes the students used in their narratives. Write them on a chart and have volunteers read their stories to the class, omitting the simile. Ask the pupils to match the similes on the chart with the paragraphs that are read aloud.

III. Lesson Conclusion

A. The students are to define the term *simile* and list the words that signal an author is using this comparative technique.

    1. Remind the students that similes make a text more descriptive and interesting.

    2. Similes compare people, places, things, and ideas that in most respects are quite different.

    3. Ask students to cite examples from their written work and from other sources.

B. Computer Connection: Ask the students to send their narratives to a relative or family friend via e-mail. Schedule class time for the students to share any interesting replies they receive.

IV. Evaluation

A. Use the discussion questions, practice exercises, and Simile Spice lesson worksheet to measure student progress and mastery.

B. Writing Applications: Use the four-point rubric scale to determine if the student *can independently, can usually,* or *requires assistance to* use similes to clarify and enhance ideas.

Simile Spice
Worksheet

*A **simile** is a figure of speech that compares two different things by using the words **like** or **as**.*

Examples: The preschool children are **as** playful **as** puppies.

Stars twinkled **like** fine jewelry in the night sky.

Exercise A

Use these incomplete phrases to create similes. Write as many words as you like.

1. Our lazy cat sleeps like _____

2. The hospital emergency room was as busy as _____

3. Autumn leaves are falling just like _____

4. On my birthday, I am as happy as _____

5. The leftover meat loaf tasted like _____

6. After work, Dad is as hungry as a _____

7. Four sprinters left the starting line like _____

8. Racecar engines roared as loud as _____

9. The deep ocean floor looks like _____

10. Those roses smell as sweet as _____

Exercise B

Read each simile. Underline what is being compared, and then choose the best meaning.

11. Air force jets soared like eagles in the blue sky.

   a. The jets are sleek and fast.

   b. The jets were chasing eagles.

   c. The jets have powerful engines.

12. My feet are frozen like the North Pole.

   a. I have extremely big feet.

   b. I am standing on my tiptoes.

   c. I need to wear better shoes and heavier socks.

Marvelous Metaphors

A second figure of speech that compares two things that appear to be quite different is the metaphor. A writer uses metaphors to create fresh, colorful word pictures in the imagination of a reader. Metaphors imply or say one person, place, thing, or idea is something else without using the terms *like* or *as*. Intermediate students require repeated practice, first with identifying and defining this figure of speech and then with its application in writing descriptively. This lesson is designed to provide the necessary drill and practice and then asks the students to use metaphors to add details to their expository writing.

Goal:

The students will use metaphors to clarify and enhance their expository writings.

Objectives:

1. Given a list of metaphors, students will read and discuss their meanings and then use them to create original examples.

2. Students will each write a friendly letter that includes a metaphor.

Materials:

- Marvelous Metaphors worksheet (page 70)
- stationery

Procedure:

I. Lesson Introduction

A. Introduce metaphors. Restate that authors use figures of speech to add details to their writing and to make the text more interesting. A metaphor compares things by implying or saying they are something else. Unlike similes, metaphors do not use the signal words *like*, *as*, *than*, or *resembles*. Often, a linking verb is a clue that an author is using a metaphor.

B. Write the following examples on the chalkboard. Ask the students to identify what is being compared. Point out the linking verbs or other clues that signal that it is a metaphor. Discuss how the phrase makes a reader see something in a different way.

   1. That warm jacket is an old friend.

   2. Sunrise was an explosion of red and gold.

C. Distribute the Marvelous Metaphors worksheet. Two more samples of this figure of speech are given, and these can be used to reinforce the lesson concept. Guide the pupils through Exercise A and have them share the metaphors they create. Exercise B will be helpful to confirm whether the students understand the meanings of metaphors in context.

Marvelous Metaphors *(cont.)*

II. Lesson Body

A. Writing Applications: Students are to create a metaphor or use one from the lesson exercises for the writing application. Students will be composing a friendly letter about an occurrence at school. A metaphor may be placed anywhere within the body of the letter, but it might fit best in the first or last sentence.

B. Prewriting: Instruct the pupils to choose one person to whom they will write. Cousins, aunts, uncles, grandparents, and neighbors always enjoy a friendly letter. Once the audience has been identified, direct the pupils to select a topic that will interest that person—one that will be exciting to share. Here are a few suggestions.

1. Write about a club or recent project.

   "I was the Einstein of our school's science fair."

2. Tell about a field trip experience.

   "All the kids on the bus were excited puppies."

3. Discuss a school team or the last game played.

   "Our quarterback is a sly fox on third down."

4. Explain about a contest you entered.

   "My free throws were rainbows, and the basket was a pot of gold."

5. Describe your teacher.

   "My math teacher is a brain."

C. Writing: Review the format of a friendly letter, including the heading, greeting, body, closing, and signature (page 69). Instruct the pupils to write the letter as if they were speaking to the reader. Be sure the purpose of the letter is stated in the first few sentences.

1. The letter must explain why the student is writing.

2. Instruct the pupils to think and answer the questions *who, what, where, when, how,* and *why* as they write their messages.

3. Highlight the sentence that contains the metaphor.

D. Revising: Have the students read their rough drafts into a tape recorder. Ask them if they like the sound of their letters and if they noticed any repetitive language that needs to be edited. The playbacks should sound friendly and natural. The body must be informative and interesting. Proofread for proper capitalization, punctuation, spelling, and grammar.

E. Publishing: Students are to make neat, legible, and correct copies of their letters. It is more appropriate to handwrite a friendly letter than to type it. The message is supposed to be informal.

1. Review how to address an envelope (page 69). Students are to address, stamp, and mail their final copies.

2. Schedule time for the pupils to share any responses they receive after mailing their letters. The best way to get a letter is to first send one.

Marvelous Metaphors *(cont.)*

III. Lesson Conclusion

A. The students are to use their own words to define the term *metaphor* and to explain the purpose of metaphors.

    1. Remind the students that metaphors add description and make the text more interesting.

    2. Metaphors compare people, places, things, and ideas that in most respects are quite different.

    3. Ask students to cite examples from their written work and from other sources.

B. Computer Connection: **"Mail Merge"** is a useful option of many word-processing programs. Prepare a sample letter and create a database using the names and addresses supplied by the students (from their friendly letter project). Explain the basic purpose of this data integration technique. With the pupils, open the database and sample letter, and then demonstrate how to merge and print documents. Ask volunteers to list five applications for this program in school, business, and at home.

IV. Evaluation

A. Use the discussion questions, practice exercises, and Marvelous Metaphors worksheet to measure student progress and mastery.

B. Writing Applications: Use the four-point rubric scale to determine if each student *can independently, can usually,* or *requires assistance to* use metaphors that clarify and enhance ideas.

How to Address an Envelope

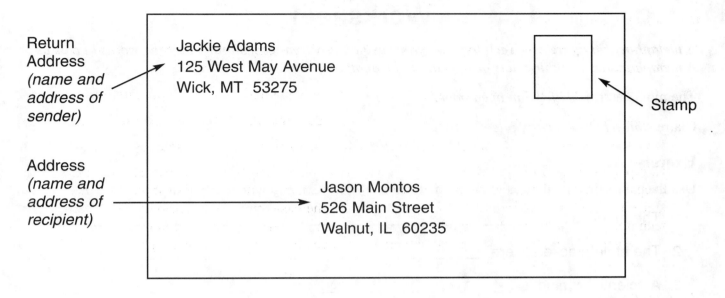

Return Address *(name and address of sender)*

Jackie Adams
125 West May Avenue
Wick, MT 53275

Stamp

Address *(name and address of recipient)*

Jason Montos
526 Main Street
Walnut, IL 60235

How to Write a Friendly Letter

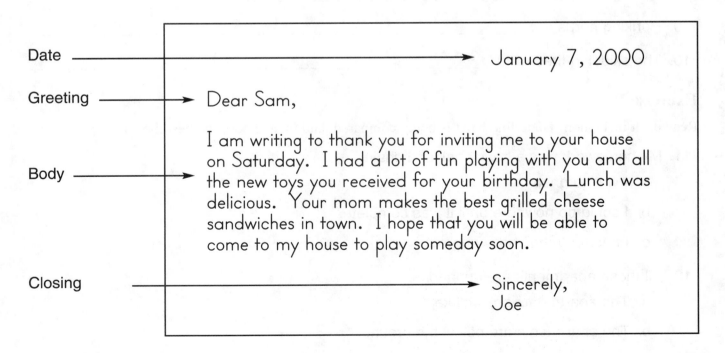

Date ——————————→ January 7, 2000

Greeting ——————→ Dear Sam,

Body ——————————→ I am writing to thank you for inviting me to your house on Saturday. I had a lot of fun playing with you and all the new toys you received for your birthday. Lunch was delicious. Your mom makes the best grilled cheese sandwiches in town. I hope that you will be able to come to my house to play someday soon.

Closing ——————————→ Sincerely,
Joe

Marvelous Metaphors
Worksheet

*A **metaphor** is a figure of speech that compares two different things **without using** the words **like** or **as**. A metaphor says one thing acts or appears to be another.*

The movie actress's *life* is *an open book.*

Claire's *bicycle* was a *rusty pile of junk.*

Exercise A

Use these incomplete phrases to create metaphors. Write as many words as you like.

1. The moon is _____

2. The stale crackers were _____

3. A scientist's mind is _____

4. The dirty fishbowl was _____

5. A flexible gymnast is _____

6. The cries of the tiny baby were _____

7. Planet Mars is _____

8. The tight necktie was _____

9. Honking horns are _____

10. The skidding tires were _____

Exercise B

Read each metaphor. Underline what is being compared, and then choose the best meaning.

11. My homework was a heavy ball and chain.

    a. I was in prison.

    b. I could go nowhere until it was complete.

    c. I had too many heavy books.

12. All these apartments are dungeons.

    a. The apartments are well kept.

    b. The apartments are below the ground.

    c. The apartments are cold and dark.

Personification Motivation

A third figure of speech often employed by writers of adolescent literature is *personification*. Objects, animals, or ideas are given human characteristics to help the readers visualize what is being described. "The walls have ears," "A magazine grabbed my attention" and "Every picture tells a story" are some basic examples. These phrases get the audience to look at ordinary situations in new and unique ways. Personification is yet another technique an author can use to make a composition original, interesting, and descriptive. The purpose of this lesson is to provide students opportunities to identify and create personification and then apply it to expository writing.

Goal:

The students will use personification to clarify and enhance their expository writing.

Objectives:

1. Given a statement of personification, students will read and determine its meaning. They will then use personification to create original sentences.
2. Students will each write a descriptive paragraph that includes an example of personification.

Materials:

- Personification Motivation worksheet (pages 74 and 75)

Procedure:

I. Lesson Introduction:

A. Introduce the term *personification*. Inform the students that authors use personification to help readers visualize what is being described by giving animals, objects, and ideas human qualities.

    1. The most common example of personification is talking animals in stories and cartoons.

    2. Personification often occurs in poetry to help readers see ordinary things in new or unique ways.

B. Write the following examples on the chalkboard. Ask the pupils to identify what human characteristic an object appears to have and direct volunteers to explain what the sentence is trying to imply.

    1. An old jalopy choked and wheezed as it climbed the steep hill.

    2. The crickets asked questions all night long.

    3. A rock went screaming past my head.

    4. Fear slowly crept in and captured its next victim.

Personification Motivation *(cont.)*

C. Distribute the Personification Motivation worksheet. Students will first be presented with examples of personification in context. They are asked to locate the figure of speech and identify its meaning. Exercise B gives a writing prompt, and the students are to create their own sentences to demonstrate their knowledge of the personification technique.

II. Lesson Body

A. Writing Applications: Students will apply personification while simulating and writing an interview with a family pet or other familiar animal. The composition will have three parts: an introduction that describes the subject being interviewed, five questions with the animal's responses, and a conclusion that summarizes and brings the interview to a close.

B. Prewriting: Present the following question to the learners: "If your pet could talk, what would you ask it?" Encourage them to use the question words *who, what, where, when,* and *how*. They will need to think of five questions to include as part of their composition. Some examples include the following:

1. What do you do all day while I am at school?
2. Where is your favorite place to lie down?
3. What do you and your friends talk about?
4. How do you like the food we feed you?
5. Who is your favorite family member?

C. Writing

1. Students will each write a descriptive paragraph as an introduction to the interview. The topic sentence will identify the animal, and the supporting sentences will detail its size, color, and any other important features or traits.

2. The middle section will contain the interviewer's questions followed by the animal's remarks. Questions with *yes* or *no* answers are to be avoided. The animal's responses may be longer than one sentence.

3. The concluding paragraph should summarize the interview's main points. A final comment about the animal's future hopes and dreams might serve as a good ending.

D. Revising

1. Students are to choose partners and role-play their rough drafts. Tell them to pretend and act as if it were a television news program interview. The story must be smooth and the questions asked in a logical order. Add details to make the questions and answers interesting. Delete unnecessary or repetitive ideas.

2. Proofread for proper capitalization, punctuation, spelling, and grammar. Students need to make sure all three of these elements are present: an introduction, the interview, and a conclusion.

Personification Motivation *(cont.)*

E. Publishing: Students are to make corrected copies of their compositions and then assemble these into a bound collection. Have volunteers create a cover and decorate it with pictures and other eye-catching visuals. Place it in the school library for others to read and enjoy.

III. Lesson Conclusion

A. Student are to define *personification* and tell why an author or poet would use this descriptive technique.

1. Remind the pupils that personification helps readers visualize what exactly is being described.

2. Personification allows readers to see ordinary objects in new or unique ways.

3. Ask students to cite examples of this figure of speech in their own written work and from other sources.

B. Computer Connection: Instruct the students to search through the "Clip Art" feature installed with most word-processing programs. Many of these prepared graphics use personification techniques for humor and attention. Print some samples, and see if the pupils can explain the uses and purposes of these pieces of artwork.

IV. Evaluation

A. Use the discussion questions, practice exercises, and the Personification Motivation worksheet to measure student progress and mastery.

B. Writing Applications: Use the four-point rubric scale to determine if each student *can independently, can usually,* or *requires assistance to* use personification to clarify and enhance ideas.

Personification Motivation
Worksheet

Personification is a figure of speech that portrays an animal, object, or idea as if it had human qualities.

Exercise A

Read each sentence. **Underline** the **personification**, and then **circle** the sentence that best gives the real meaning of this figure of speech.

1. An old jalopy gagged and wheezed as it tried to climb the steep hill.
   a. The car's driver was choking.
   b. The car has run over something in the road.
   c. The car's motor is making a lot of noise.

2. Curiosity ate away at Denise until she finally asked if the winning ticket was hers.
   a. Denise has a terrible skin disease.
   b. Denise could not stop thinking about her ticket.
   c. Denise was being chewed upon by an animal.

3. Fog huddled about all along the docks of the bay.
   a. You could not see the water because of the fog.
   b. You are at a football game near a lake.
   c. You are out in the rain without an umbrella.

4. Gusty winds made a leaf pile hop, skip, and jump.
   a. The leaves are blowing around.
   b. The leaves are dancing in the street.
   c. The leaves are being raked.

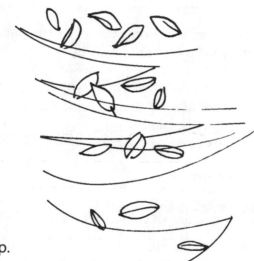

5. The cave seemed to yawn as explorers went inside.
   a. The explorers were very tired.
   b. The explorers were searching for a place to camp.
   c. The explorers were going through a large opening.

6. Prickly bushes grabbed at me as I walked through the thick weeds.
   a. There were prickly bushes that had claws.
   b. There were a lot of sharp, prickly bushes.
   c. There were evil people hiding in the weeds.

7. There is not much traffic in that sleepy little town.
   a. The town is far away from the major highways.
   b. The townspeople are good sleepers.
   c. The town has no roads.

8. That telephone appears to be Claire's best friend.
   a. Claire is always talking on the phone.
   b. Claire works for the phone company.
   c. Claire makes friends very easily.

Personification Motivation
Worksheet *(cont.)*

Exercise B

Think of a human quality these objects, animals, and ideas could have. Use personification and write a sentence.

9. a very dim light bulb _____

_____

_____

10. a famous oil painting _____

_____

_____

11. a sleek red sports car _____

_____

_____

12. an old stuffed chair _____

_____

_____

13. an overflowing trash can _____

_____

_____

14. windshield wipers _____

_____

_____

15. an ambulance siren _____

_____

_____

16. a telephone busy signal _____

_____

_____

17. a midnight campfire _____

_____

_____

18. thunder and lightning _____

_____

Types
of
Paragraphs

76
©Teacher Created Materials, Inc.

The Explanatory Paragraph

The explanatory, or "how to," paragraph is also known as the process essay. Recipes, game rules, set-up instructions, machine operation, and directions given by a teacher are common examples we read and follow daily. Cookbooks, diet journals, and do-it-yourself manuals are numerous in our home libraries. One method of learning how to carefully follow directions is to practice composing them. This lesson is designed to guide the students and help them create this type of instructional paragraph.

Goal:

Students will prewrite, write, revise, and publish an explanatory paragraph.

Objectives:

1. Students will practice writing sentences using words and phrases that signal step-by-step instructions.
2. Given a topic sentence, students will list related events in proper time-order sequence.

Materials:

- Guidelines for Writing an Explanatory Paragraph (page 80)
- Explanatory Paragraph worksheet (pages 81 and 82)

Procedure:

I. Lesson Introduction

A. Begin the lesson with a discussion about household devices that need an explanation in order to be used properly. A good example to prompt the class is a washing machine. List the following basic steps on the chalkboard:

   1. Put in detergent.

   2. Set the dials and switches.

   3. Add dirty clothes.

   4. Start the cycle.

   Talk about the importance of following the list in the correct order. Have pupils share their ideas about comical or ruinous events that could occur if the directions were out of sequence. Ask volunteers to supply an appropriate topic sentence and concluding statement. End this discussion by having one pupil recite all the sentences together as a paragraph.

The Explanatory Paragraph *(cont.)*

B. Introduce the concept of time-order words. Some common choices are *first, next, then, after that,* and *finally*. Refer to the paragraph about how to wash a load of dirty clothes. Insert these step-by-step signal words into the list above, then reread the sentences. Point out that these terms help provide a smooth transition from one idea to the next and help a writer organize the directions in a logical order.

C. Distribute the Explanatory Paragraph worksheet. The first exercise presents the learners with an explanatory paragraph. Students are to read it, then add time-order words to make the main idea clear and complete. The second task requires pupils to reorder given sentences and write them as an explanatory paragraph. The time-order words serve as clues to its sequence. Tell the students to refer to this worksheet as they write and revise their own explanatory paragraphs.

II. Lesson Body

A. Writing Application: Students are to choose a topic and create an explanatory paragraph. Current science, social studies, math, and reading lessons may be a good source of ideas. Give each writer a copy of the Guidelines for Writing an Explanatory Paragraph (page 80) and review the four steps of the writing process.

B. Prewriting: Encourage the students to choose a topic they are interested in and familiar with. Instruct them to create two lists: one that contains any necessary materials (dirty clothes, detergent, washing machine) and another that orders the steps (first, next, then, after that, last). Tell the pupils to identify their audience because often younger readers require more direct and exact information in the supporting sentences.

C. Writing: Topic sentences state what is being explained. Students are to follow this statement with one that lists what is needed to perform the task. The supporting details will be the step-by-step instructions. Conclude with a sentence that informs the reader that he or she has successfully completed the process. Offer the following topic sentences to prompt the writers. Notice how a variety of sentence types is employed.

1. This is how to make the best fried bologna sandwich in the world!

2. After reading this, you will be able to build a better go-cart.

3. Follow these instructions and learn how to play the card game "Old Maid."

4. Do you know how to set the timer on your microwave oven?

5. Starting a lawn mower is easy if you follow these steps.

The Explanatory Paragraph (cont.)

D. Revising

   1. Direct the writers to test their written directions. All the crucial steps must be present and in proper order. Ask an adult to mirror the process as the instructions are read aloud. Instruct the pupils to listen for repetitive language and replace it with nifty nouns, vivid verbs, exact adjectives, and interesting adverbs.

   2. Proofread for correct capitalization, punctuation, spelling, and grammar. Allow the students to use a word-processing program to produce a final copy. Any paragraphs that are hand-written must be neat and legible.

E. Publishing: Assemble the paragraphs into a classroom "How to . . . Encyclopedia." Have volunteers design a cover, a table of contents, and an index. (See page 114 for samples of these pages.) Make copies of this volume available to other writers and the building media center.

III. Lesson Conclusion

A. Students are to state the purpose of an explanatory paragraph and recite the five basic guidelines for writing this type of composition.

   1. Review and list the common time-order words and define their use.

   2. Restate the four steps of the writing process and ask volunteers to explain the function of each one.

B. Computer Connection: Have the students bring in the instruction manuals to some of their favorite software programs. Schedule class time and ask the pupils to read aloud an explanatory section from these booklets. Instruct the listeners to note time-order words when they are heard.

IV. Evaluation

A. Use the discussion questions, practice paragraphs, and explanatory worksheet to measure student progress and mastery.

B. Writing Applications: Use the four-point rubric scale to determine if each student *can independently, can usually,* or *needs assistance to* write expository compositions.

Guidelines for Writing an Explanatory Paragraph

❏ The topic sentence must state what is being explained by the paragraph.

❏ The second sentence will list all materials that will be needed.

❏ The supporting sentences will be step-by-step instruction. The signal words *first*, *next*, *then*, *after that*, and *finally* will help make the instructions exact and clear.

❏ Proofread carefully to make sure all the crucial steps have been included.

❏ Test your instructions. Revise, if necessary.

The Explanatory Paragraph
Worksheet

*An **explanatory paragraph** informs the reader about how to make or do something.*

Exercise A

Complete the paragraph by adding the best signal words from the list below. Use each word only once although you will find that some sentences could be completed with more than one of the signal words.

Signal Words		
after that	at last	next
then	first	finally

Make a Cloud

Follow these instructions, and you can make a cloud.

_____, you need a wide-mouth jar, a flashlight, one cup of

hot water, and a tray of ice cubes. _____, pour the hot

water into the jar. _____, take the jar to a darkroom or closet.

_____, place the tray of ice cubes on top of the jar.

_____, shine the flashlight towards the middle of the jar.

_____, you will see a small cloud appear inside the jar.

The Explanatory Paragraph
Worksheet *(cont.)*

Exercise B

On the lines provided below, write the following sentences as an explanatory paragraph. Write the topic sentence first. Then, put the other sentences in the correct order. Finally, give it a title.

1. Then, press the sponge into the ink pad.
2. Next, hold the leaf firmly against the paper.
3. Let the ink dry, and display your picture.
4. Do you know how to make a leaf silhouette?
5. After that, carefully remove the leaf.
6. Begin by gathering a leaf, white paper, a sponge, and an ink pad.
7. Rub the sponge all around the leaf edges with outward strokes.

Writing Directions

Another composition process is one that lists directions from a starting point to a final destination. Young people hear and are asked to give directions constantly during their day. Therefore, drill and practice are necessary in order to write or recite them accurately. Since world interactions and map skills are such an important part of the intermediate curriculum, pupils need to understand how to write directions that can be clearly understood and easily followed. This lesson is designed to guide students in creating this type of instructional paragraph.

Goal:

Students will prewrite, write, revise, and publish a set of directions.

Objectives:

1. Students will practice writing sentences using words and phrases that indicate direction or location.

2. Given a set of vague or unclear directions, students will add the names of people, places, and things to make them more exact.

Materials:

- local, national, and international maps
- Common Rules to Follow When Writing Directions (page 86)
- Writing Directions worksheet (page 87)

Procedure:

I. Lesson Introduction

A. Break into small groups. Assign a location to each group. Have the group work together to write simple directions to their location. They may need to consult maps or an atlas. After a period of time, bring the class back together. Have each group read their directions, and have the class try to identify the place described.

B. Have two volunteers leave the room or go out of hearing range. Lead a class discussion and create a set of directions that will have one of the volunteers go to a specific place in the building and perform a specific task (e.g., walk to the office and make a PA announcement). Use the chalkboard or overhead projector to record the student-generated supporting sentences. Proofread, revise, and have a student copy the directions onto a card. Call in the first volunteer, and test out the instructions. Upon this person's return, revise one more time, and then test the final copy on the second volunteer.

Writing Directions *(cont.)*

C. Spend a few minutes evaluating these activities. Ask the students to identify what parts of their instructions were unclear or difficult to follow. Review how the class revised and rewrote them to make the directions more accurate and understandable. Introduce the concept of directional words. Explain that terms such as *east, west, across, straight, front,* and *end* help make directions specific and exact.

D. Distribute the Writing Directions worksheet. Exercise A presents a list of vague directions. The students are to rewrite them and add directional words to make these phrases more exact. Exercise B requires the students to replace vague or unclear words with more specific names of people, places, or things in order to make the directions accurate.

II. Lesson Body

A. Writing Applications: Students are to write an accurate set of directions that explain how to get from their home to school. Give each writer a copy of the Common Rules to Follow When Writing Directions and review the four steps of the writing process.

B. Prewriting: First the students must mentally organize and plan their routes; then, they should sketch a map. Assist them by naming a few reference points to help them locate north, south, east, and west. Direct the pupils to make a list of street names and the number of right and left turns. A local political map or street map will be a useful aid.

C. Writing: The first sentence explains the purpose of the directions. Students are to refer to their sketches and other notes they took during the prewriting step as they compose the supporting sentences. Review imperative sentences and cite a few practice examples to help the students get off to a good start. Instruct the pupils to limit the number of details. Not every twist and turn needs to be mentioned.

❏ Turn right onto Telegraph Road.

❏ Go two miles until Phillips Street.

❏ Head north four city blocks.

❏ Cross over the pedestrian bridge.

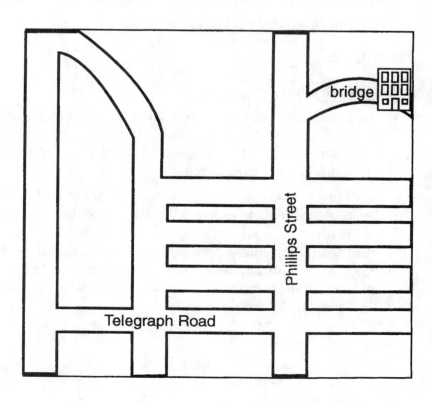

Writing Directions *(cont.)*

D. Revising

    1. The paragraphs must be evaluated for reasonable accuracy, clarity, and completeness. Direction signal words and phrases will make each command more exact. Specific street names, building numbers, and other points of interest will give the paragraph more description. Addresses, directional words, and distances need to be double-checked.

    2. Proofread for proper capitalization, punctuation, spelling, and grammar. It is generally a good idea to check one of these elements at a time. Also, instruct the students to work backwards. Sometimes if one starts at the end and moves to the beginning, errors are easier to spot.

E. Publishing: Post a map of your town or school district on a bulletin board, and then surround it with corrected copies of the students' compositions. Students may include pictures of their homes as visuals. Color-code and draw arrows from the papers to the described locations on the map. Remember to highlight the position of your school building.

III. Lesson Conclusion

A. Students are to state the purpose for being specific when writing or giving directions. Have them list a number of the directional signal words and phrases. Instruct volunteers to recite the five basic rules to follow when writing or giving directions.

    1. Together, brainstorm a list of careers in which accurate destination directions are important.

    2. End the lesson with a discussion about the consequences of inaccurate or incorrect directions.

B. Computer Connection: There are numerous locator and mapping sites on the Internet (e.g., *www.maps.com*). Schedule time in your school's computer lab, and let the pupils look up maps and information concerning out-of-town relatives, family vacations, or places their parents have traveled to for business reasons.

IV. Evaluation

A. Use the discussion questions, practice exercises, and Writing Directions worksheet to measure student progress and mastery.

B. Writing Applications: Use the four-point rubric scale to determine if each student *can independently, can usually,* or *needs assistance to* write expository compositions.

Common Rules to Follow When Writing Directions

❏ A topic sentence explains the purpose of the directions.

❏ Supporting sentences must follow a logical, first-to-last order.

❏ The signal words and phrases—*north, south, left, right, across from, straight, in back, up,* and *down*—are key terms that clarify directions.

❏ The inclusion of the names of streets, buildings, parks, and other landmarks is a necessary component of good direction writing.

❏ House addresses and building numbers need to be double-checked during proofreading.

Writing Directions
Worksheet

Be specific and use **signal words and phrases** *when writing or giving directions.*

Exercise A

Rewrite each sentence, and make the directions exact by adding the best signal word from the list below. Use each word only once, although you will find that some sentences could be completed with more than one of the signal words.

Signal Words

right

up

down

north

in front

1. Turn at the next stoplight.

   _____

2. The arrow is pointing.

   _____

3. Hiram Village is that way from here.

   _____

4. Take the elevator to the parking garage.

   _____

5. This store has plenty of parking there.

   _____

Exercise B

Read and then rewrite. Make these directions more exact by adding the names of people, places, and things to each sentence.

6. The construction on *this road* makes it impossible to go straight.

   _____

7. *That amusement park* is ten miles southwest of *here*.

   _____

8. If you look to the left, you will see *it*.

   _____

9. *Those shops* are directly across the *street*.

   _____

10. I found a *bunch of these* behind the store.

    _____

Standards and Benchmarks: 1A, 1B, 1C, 1E, 1F, 1G, 1I, 1J, 2A, 2B, 2C, 3A, 3B, 3C, 3D, 3E, 3F, 3G, 3H, 3I, 3J, 3K, 3L

The Cause-and-Effect Paragraph

As students reach the age of adolescence, they must begin to look at the "big picture" and the part their daily lives play in relation to it. During the elementary years, family, friends, and classmates are the center of a child's attention. Intermediate students begin to have these private worlds invaded with current events, politics, and economics. Students start to realize that thoughts and actions are influenced by information from beyond their local, safe environment. This lesson is designed to have the learners recognize and write about cause-effect relationships.

Goal:

Students will prewrite, write, revise, and publish a cause-and-effect paragraph.

Objectives:

1. Given a set of events, the students will identify the causes and effects.

2. Students will locate cause-and-effect relationships in an expository writing sample.

Materials:

- cause-and-effect worksheet (pages 91 and 92)
- cause-and-effect expository sample (page 93)

Procedure:

I. Lesson Introduction

A. Cause: Inform the students that a cause is a condition or action that brings about other events. Ask the students to think of times when they had to practice a task. List these tasks, and then ask the pupils why practice was necessary and crucial. Inquire into the results of the practice and reasons why it was positive or negative. Tell the group that the practice was one of the causes of the final outcome. Some prompts to start the students thinking follow:

    1. practice for a sporting event

    2. studying for a test

    3. rehearsing music, dance, or drama

The Cause-and-Effect Paragraph *(cont.)*

B. Effect: The effect is the result of one condition/action or a series of condition/actions. This reaction, or outcome, occurs because one or more events came first. Ask the students to think of performances, tests, or competitions in which they took part. These culminating activities were the effects of all the practice, study, and rehearsing that came before them. Some prompts to start the students thinking:

    1. a championship soccer match

    2. a grade-level proficiency test

    3. a piano recital

C. Usually, one cause can have several effects, and one effect might have been the result of several causes. At the intermediate level, start with the basic one cause/one effect scenario. As the students progress toward mastery, feel free to complicate matters and expand the cause-and-effect situations.

D. Signal Words: On the chalkboard, list the following words and phrases that signal cause-and-effect relationships: *as, because, since, so, therefore, thus, due to, as a result of,* and *consequently.* Remind the students that, as in paragraphs of contrast, signal words clarify ideas, provide a smooth transition from one detail to the next, and help the reader recognize cause-and-effect relationships. Create a poster of these terms and decorate it with picture cut outs that imply cause-and-effect relationships. The computer connection activities on page 90 offer another strategy for practicing, drilling, and displaying these necessary words.

II. Lesson Body

A. Prewriting: There are two worksheets that offer practice, a written example, and application of the skills necessary to write a cause-and-effect composition. Guide the students through these exercises, with the goal in mind that a topic to write about is needed.

B. Writing: Once a topic has been identified, some organization will be required. Before the first draft is written, the students must decide the main idea for their topic sentences.

    1. If the topic sentence explains a cause, the supporting sentences will detail the results or effects.

    2. If the topic sentence explains an effect, the supporting sentences will detail why this event happened or its causes.

    3. Students can refer to the lesson worksheets for guidance and must remember to use words and terms that signal cause-and-effect relationships.

C. Proofreading and Revising: Peer editing is a very effective strategy to use while revising a cause-and-effect paragraph. Allow time for the pupils to trade their rough drafts and to comment on each other's initial efforts. *"This is what I liked best about your paper . . ."* and *"I need to know more about . . ."* are two responses to start with. Most compositions will have main ideas which classmates can share and have opinions about. In addition to proofreading for capitalization, punctuation, grammar, and spelling errors, the editors must help the writer revise and avoid overusing some words.

The Cause and Effect Paragraph (cont.)

D. Publishing:

    1. After the students have written and shared their final drafts, choose two or three that can be acted out as cause-and-effect skits. Organize the students into small groups, give them copies of the original cause-and-effect paragraphs, and have the groups improvise one-act plays.

    2. Choose one cause-and-effect composition and have one group perform a skit as the material was written. Ask the others to create different or unexpected endings to theirs. These new twists to the main idea can be serious or comical.

III. Lesson Conclusion

A. The students must be able to state that a cause-and-effect relationship exists when one condition causes another to happen.

    1. Recognizing cause-and-effect relationships helps make clear to a reader why certain events occur.

    2. Recognizing cause-and-effect relationships is a critical skill necessary for the comprehension of nonfiction.

    3. Students also must be able to list the words and phrases that signal a cause-effect relationship.

B. Computer Connection:

    1. Instruct the pupils to use a word-processing program to produce their final copies of their cause-and-effect paragraphs. Have them use bold or italic type to highlight the cause-effect signal words as they occur in the paragraph.

    2. Make a banner of the cause-and-effect signal words and phrases. Use it as part of a bulletin board that displays the students' cause-effect paragraphs.

IV. Evaluation

A. Use the discussion questions, practice exercises, and signal words and phrases worksheets to measure student progress and mastery.

B. Writing Applications: Use the four-point rubric scale to determine if each student *can independently, can usually,* or *needs assistance to* write cause-and-effect compositions.

The Cause-and-Effect Paragraph
Worksheet #1

*A **cause-effect** composition explains why an event occurred by telling the results of an action.*

Exercise A

List five possible causes for each of the following events.

1. A teenager is grounded for a whole week.

   _____

   _____

   _____

   _____

2. Several farm animals have wandered away from the farm.

   _____

   _____

   _____

   _____

3. Local police officers have closed a bridge.

   _____

   _____

   _____

   _____

4. A short boy is made captain of the basketball team.

   _____

   _____

   _____

   _____

5. The soloist did not make a mistake during the recital.

   _____

   _____

   _____

   _____

The Cause-and-Effect Paragraph
Worksheet #1 *(cont.)*

Exercise B

List five possible effects of each of the following events.

1. There was a half-hour wait to ride a roller coaster.

   _____

   _____

   _____

   _____

2. The working conditions at a local construction site were unsafe.

   _____

   _____

   _____

   _____

3. A pan of broccoli was left unattended, cooking on the stove.

   _____

   _____

   _____

   _____

4. A toddler has Dad's car keys.

   _____

   _____

   _____

   _____

5. Rain was forecast for the day of the class picnic.

   _____

   _____

   _____

   _____

The Cause-and-Effect Paragraph
Worksheet #2

*A **cause-and-effect** composition explains why an event occurred by telling the results of an action.*

Read the cause-and-effect article. Note signal words and the events of the story. Choose the best answer to each question below.

A violent hurricane hit the mainland just before suppertime. Gale-force winds, 12-foot waves, and severe thunderstorms blasted away cottages along the boardwalk. The weather bureau had warned that the storm was coming, and most of the residents had left town.

Fred McCord was very foolish—but lucky—that day. He knew that the storm was brewing so he decided to go to the beach. The ocean waves seemed perfect for some daredevil surfing. Fred was having a wonderful time when a civil defense patrol volunteer spotted him in the water. A police officer was called, and he quickly escorted Fred out of the area and into a shelter.

After 48 hours, local people were allowed to go back to their homes. The Freedmans had left town days before as the storm approached. They had boarded up all the windows and taken other safety precautions. Sadly, when they reached their lot, they discovered only a foundation full of debris.

1. Which of the following caused all the damage?
   a. the residents of the town
   b. daredevil surfing
   c. a violent hurricane
   d. civil defense patrol volunteers

2. Which of the following was not the result of the hurricane?
   a. the Freedman's house being destroyed
   b. a police officer escorting Fred from the beach
   c. residents not warned
   d. gale-force winds and 12-foot waves

3. Describe how you would react to a severe storm. (If you have lived through a hurricane or tornado, write about your experience.)

_____

_____

_____

_____

_____

The Contrast Paragraph

The intermediate student is at an age in which the powers of observation must be exercised in order to recognize the differences among people, places, things, and ideas. This skill will be called upon numerous times during science and social studies as the lessons compare and contrast the human condition and our environment. Young people need to practice organizing these observations and stringing them together in a logical manner. This lesson is designed to have the students apply the four-step writing process to compose a paragraph of contrast.

Goal:

The students will prewrite, write, revise, and publish a contrast paragraph.

Objectives:

1. Given a topic sentence, students will work cooperatively and brainstorm a list of supporting details.

2. Students will write sentences using words and phrases that signal a contrasting relationship.

Materials:

- The Contrast Paragraph worksheet (page 96)

Procedure:

I. Lesson Introduction

A. Ask the students to list ways that bicycles can be different. Have them discuss and identify the most significant characteristic that can make one bike unlike another. Organize the list, add a topic sentence and a concluding sentence, and then recite this contrast paragraph. Repeat this exercise with other topics, such as video game systems, pizza, coaches, and superheroes.

B. Explain that identifying how people, places, things, and ideas are different exercises thinking skills and improves one's powers of observation. A contrast paragraph is one way an author communicates and points out differences.

II. Lesson Body

A. Introduce the concept of signal words and phrases. These terms clarify ideas, provide a smooth transition from one detail to the next, and help the reader understand how ideas and details fit together.

1. The Contrast Paragraph worksheet offers students an opportunity to practice using signal words and phrases.

2. Exercise A requires the learners to use words and phrases that signal a contrasting relationship to complete a variety of sentences. Then in Exercise B, an incomplete paragraph of contrast is presented, and students must add the signal words and phrases.

The Contrast Paragraph *(cont.)*

II. Lesson Body

   B. Once there has been large group practice, it is time to break off into small groups. At this point, students are to be given a topic and asked to work cooperatively, apply the four-step writing process, and create a paragraph of contrast. Some sample topics:

      1. There are many differences between beagles and basset hounds.

      2. Here are four ways cable TV and broadcast TV are not the same.

      3. Do you know how football and soccer differ?

      4. Trading cards change from year to year.

   C. Contrast Paragraph Checklist

      1. The topic sentence states what has been chosen to contrast.

      2. The supporting sentences detail the differences in a logical order.

      3. Signal words (*although, besides, even though, however, in contrast, on the other hand*) are used to combine ideas and provide a smooth transition from one sentence to the next.

      4. A conclusion sentence restates the topic and sums up the main idea.

      5. The paper is proofread for proper grammer, capitalization, punctuation, spelling, and legibility.

      6. A neat and corrected copy of the composition is ready to share with the intended audience.

III. Lesson Conclusion

   A. Review the purpose of contrast paragraphs.

      1. Contrast paragraphs point out the differences among people, places, things, and ideas.

      2. Contrast paragraphs offer a chance to apply and practice one's power of observation in a meaningful way.

   B. Ask for volunteers to state the purpose of contrast signal words and phrases, and then list them orally or on the chalkboard.

   C. Restate the four steps of the writing process. Making a two-column chart and listing contrasting characteristics is a helpful method for organizing a paragraph of contrast.

   D. Writing Applications: Members are to make their own copies of their group's final effort. Have them compare the writings and point out any significant differences in content or style.

   E. Publishing

      1. Instruct the students to cut and paste pictures that represent the topics of contrast presented in their compositions. Display these together on a bulletin board.

      2. Computer Connection: Instruct the students to use a word-processing program to produce their final drafts. Have each group member choose a different font. Print the compositions and display them side by side—the messages will be similar, but the appearances will contrast.

IV. Evaluation:

   A. Use the guided practice, discussion questions, and worksheet to measure student progress and mastery.

   B. Writing Applications: Use the four-point rubric scale to determine if each student *can independently*, *can usually*, or *needs assistance to* write expository compositions of contrast.

The Contrast Paragraph
Worksheet

*A **contrast paragraph** presents details about the differences between objects, persons, places, or ideas.*

Exercise A

Complete each sentence by adding the best signal word from the list below. Use each word only once although you will find that some sentences could be completed with more than one of the signal words.

Signal Words		
while	however	or
not	difference	unlike

1. This is how to tell the _____ between roses and carnations.

2. Roses have thorns, and carnations do _____.

3. One has smooth pedals, _____ the other's are jagged.

4. A rose's leaves have rounded edges; _____, the leaves of a carnation are longer and pointy.

5. _____ carnations, roses grow as a bush.

6. Which flower do you prefer, roses _____ carnations?

Exercise B

Complete the paragraph by adding the best signal words from the list below. Use each word only once although you will find that some sentences could be completed with more than one of the signal words.

Signal Words		
while	different	in contrast
unlike		not the same

Do you know how draft horses and racehorses are _____? A draft horse lives on a farm, _____ a racehorse, which lives at a track. One is tall with muscles for pulling and hauling. _____, the other is smaller and bred to run fast. Cowboys and farmers care for draft horses, _____ jockeys and trainers care for racehorses. Now you know that these two impressive animals are _____.

The Comparison Paragraph

Contrast paragraphs challenge a student's powers of observation to notice differences between people, places, things, or ideas. From afar these appear very similar, but with closer inspection they are not. Comparative writing is just the opposite. With this task, writers must exercise and focus their thinking skills to point out the ways in which two apparently unique people, places, things, or ideas have common characteristics. Pupils will have to gather information and organize their thoughts carefully in order to write meaningful paragraphs that clearly communicate their findings. This lesson is designed to help students apply the four-step writing process to create a comparative paragraph.

Goal:

The students will prewrite, write, revise, and publish a comparative paragraph.

Objectives:

1. Given a topic sentence, students will work cooperatively and brainstorm a list of supporting details.

2. Students will write sentences using words and phrases that signal a comparative relationship.

Materials:

- The Comparison Paragraph worksheet (page 100)

Procedure:

I. Lesson Introduction

A. Explain to the students that comparative paragraphs point out characteristics that unique people, places, things, or ideas have in common (for example, roller skating and skateboarding).

   1. Both are activities that require small wheels.

   2. A person needs good balance, physical strength, and endurance to be successful.

   3. Both have moves and stunts that require hours of practice to execute well.

   4. A smooth surface is necessary for each.

B. Next, work together as a large group to create a comparison paragraph. Brainstorm a list of ways hot dogs and hamburgers are similar. Use a side-by-side chart to organize these ideas. Create a topic sentence and add a concluding sentence to make the paragraph complete.

   1. Write a rough draft on the chalkboard or on an overhead projector.

   2. Proofread to eliminate errors and repetitive words.

   3. Revise and organize the supporting sentences into a logical, meaningful order.

   4. Ask a volunteer to recite the final paragraph.

The Comparison Paragraph *(cont.)*

C. The maturing intermediate child will face conflicts which they will be expected to solve with little or no adult intervention. One effective strategy is to identify the common ground when two sides seem so very far apart. Pointing out and describing similar characteristics of two or more obviously different people, places, things, or ideas is the purpose of a comparative paragraph. This type of expository writing allows students to practice their powers of observation and to express their points of view. After completing the body of this lesson, students will have practiced writing descriptively and reviewed an important problem-solving technique.

II. Lesson Body

A. Introduce the concept of words and phrases that signal that two (or more) people, places, things, or ideas are being compared. The lesson worksheet provides opportunities for the pupils to recognize and practice with many of these terms.

   1. In Exercise A, students are asked to supply a signal word or phrase to complete a given sentence.

   2. Exercise B presents a comparative paragraph, and the students must fill in signal words and phrases to make it complete.

B. Prewriting: Present the following list of main-idea sentences. The students may use them or suggest some of their own. Advise the pupils to mirror the method used when the class created a practice paragraph during the lesson introduction. Use a side-by-side chart to list similar characteristics. If they cannot think of four traits their topics have in common, a better topic is needed.

   1. Ballet and gymnastics are similar in many ways.

   2. Do you know how hurricanes and tornadoes are alike?

   3. Parents and teachers say the same things.

   4. Jokes and riddles both can make you laugh.

C. Writing: Tell the students to begin with a sentence that will capture a reader's attention. This can be declarative, interrogative, imperative, or exclamatory. The sentence must also state what unique people, places, things, or ideas are being compared.

The Comparison Paragraph *(cont.)*

    D. Revising and Proofreading: Besides looking for capitalization, punctuation, spelling, and grammar errors, attention must be made to the elements that make this a comparative paragraph. At least four common qualities need to be noted, and the supporting sentences must be organized in a meaningful manner. Offer to proofread these rough drafts for the pupils, or instruct them to have another adult read them before proceeding to the next step.

    E. Publishing: Tell the students to prepare a neat and final copy of their comparative compositions. A word-processing program may be used to create the final draft. Have them locate and include illustrations or pictures that reflect the topics of their papers. Assemble the paragraphs into a bound collection that students can refer to during future writing projects.

III. Lesson Conclusion

    A. Students must be able to define the purpose of a comparative paragraph and tell how it differs from other types of expository writing.

        1. Restate that this type of writing helps young people practice their powers of observation and thinking skills.

        2. Finding similarities is a problem-solving technique that helps students understand how supposedly different people, places, things, or ideas can have common traits.

        3. Review the list of comparative signal words and phrases. Writers use these terms to clarify ideas and details, to provide a smooth transition from one idea to the next, and to help the reader understand how the ideas fit together.

    B. Review the four-step writing process.

        1. *Prewriting:* gathering materials and writing ideas

        2. *Writing:* putting your thoughts in writing for the first time

        3. *Revising:* adding to and deleting from your writing, and then applying proofreading skills

        4. *Publishing:* making a written piece into a final product

    C. Computer Connection: Schedule time during the prewriting step for the students to explore the Internet. Instruct them to look for information related to their topics. Remind the students that their paragraphs need at least four supporting sentences that detail what the people, places, things, or ideas they have chosen have in common.

IV. Evaluation

    A. Use the discussion questions, the practice paragraph, and the lesson worksheet to measure student progress and mastery.

    B. Writing Applications: Use the four-point rubric scale to determine if each student *can independently*, *can usually*, or *needs assistance to* write a comparative composition.

The Comparison Paragraph
Worksheet

*A **comparative paragraph** presents details about the similarities between two (or more) objects, persons, places, or ideas.*

Exercise A

Complete each sentence by adding the best signal word from the list below.   Use each word only once although you will find that some sentences could be completed with more than one of the signal words.

Signal Words

also	each	in common
both	typical	similar

1. The wildlife in ponds and lakes is _____.

2. _____ place is the home of bass, blue gill, and sunfish.

3. Water striders, whirl-a-gigs, and beetles are the _____ insects found there.

4. Growing in _____ are lilies and cattails.

5. The environment in ponds and lakes is _____ ideal for frogs and turtles.

6. These are just a few of the living things ponds and lakes have _____.

Exercise B

Complete the paragraph by adding the best signal words from the list below. Use each word only once although you will find that some sentences could be completed with more than one of the signal words.

Signal Words

alike	both	in common
also	similar	likewise

Believe it or not, BMX bicycles and ATV motorcycles have a lot _____. The tires and wheels are _____ because these parts must take a pounding from jumps and landings. _____, each is equipped with heavy-duty brakes, shock absorbers, and pedals. Riders of _____ wear helmets and pads. _____, they each get covered with dirt as they ride on paths through the woods and mud. What else about BMX bicycles and ATV motorcycles are _____?

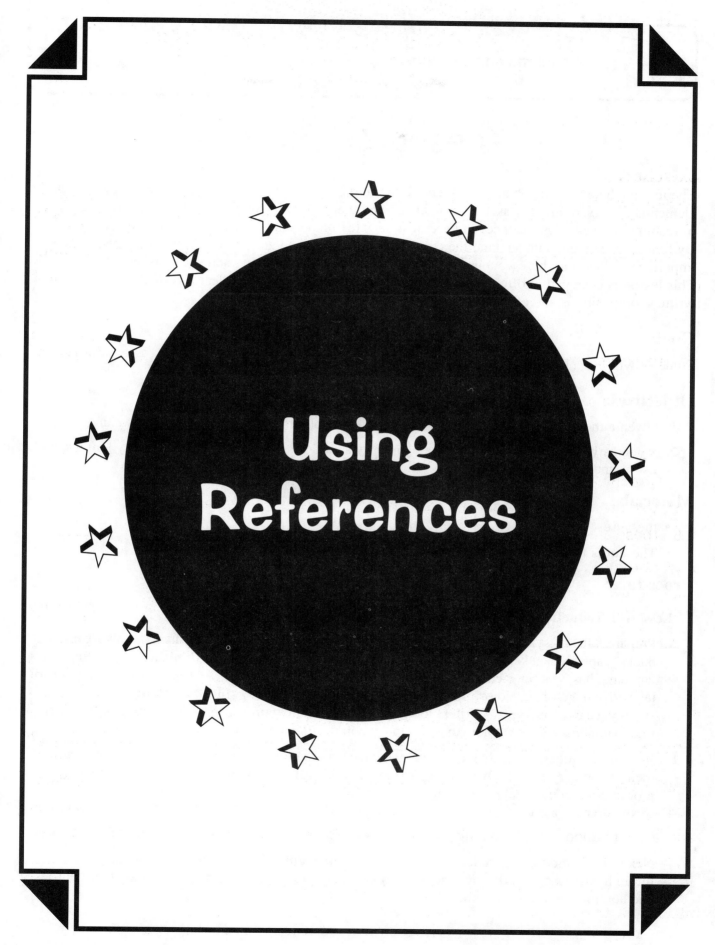

Using References

Thesaurus Power

The intermediate level is the age at which the thesaurus must be introduced and utilized. During the elementary years, dictionary skills are practiced and then applied. Next, glossaries appear in the backs of reading, mathematics, science, and social studies textbooks, and students work with these references. By fourth grade, pupils understand the concept of synonyms and antonyms. A thesaurus becomes an important tool to help these youngsters increase and refine their writing and speaking vocabularies. This lesson is designed to offer practice using a thesaurus. Students will learn to add variety to their written compositions and eliminate repetitive language while revising.

Goal:

Students will use a thesaurus when revising and rewriting compositions.

Objectives:

1. Given a thesaurus entry, the students will list and apply its synonyms to sentence writing.

2. Students will use a thesaurus to locate an entry's part of speech, definition, list of synonyms, and list of antonyms.

Materials:

- thesaurus
- Thesaurus Power worksheet (pages 104 and 105)

Procedure:

I. Lesson Introduction

A. Prepare a list of synonyms for the word "money" (e.g., dough, jack, simoleons, long green, bucks, cabbage, shekels, yellow boys, hard cash, bank, chicken feed). Explain that our English language has a larger, richer vocabulary than most other languages. A strategy to use in order to take advantage of our colorful language is to practice thesaurus skills. A thesaurus is a book of synonyms and antonyms. Writers look up common and overused words in a thesaurus in order to find synonyms. These synonyms help make compositions more interesting and less repetitive.

B. Inform the students that they are at an age where word choice is more crucial than it was during their elementary years. Overused words must be identified and modified while revising and proofreading a paragraph. Present the following list of words and have the pupils brainstorm a list of synonyms for each:

    1. good   2. nice   3. big   4. run   5. eat

Next allow time for the students to share their brainstormed lists. Finally, let the students skim through a thesaurus to discover how this book is organized. Instruct them to locate these entries and add more synonyms to their lists.

Thesaurus Power *(cont.)*

II. Lesson Body

A. Introduce the lesson worksheet. Point out that entries in most thesauruses are similar to those found in a dictionary. Each word's part of speech, definition, and a sample sentence are present. Unlike a dictionary or glossary, a thesaurus contains synonyms and antonyms for each entry. Exercise A will help students familiarize and practice basic thesaurus research skills.

B. Exercise B has students applying the entry's synonyms in context. Pupils must study each sentence carefully and choose the best synonym from the given list. By selecting the correct word, the sentence will be more exact and more descriptive.

C. Exercise C asks students to look up a given word in an actual thesaurus and then use its synonyms to improve a list of sentences. The goal is to get students to replace overused words with more interesting, higher-level synonyms.

III. Lesson Conclusion

A. Students are to state the purpose of a thesaurus and how it supplements a dictionary or glossary. They are to list the basic elements of a quality thesaurus (*entry words, part of speech, definition, sample sentences, lists of synonyms, lists of antonyms*) and tell where to find this book on the reference shelf (*in the same area as the dictionaries*).

B. Writing Applications: Students are to locate in a thesaurus a common word that has at least five listed synonyms. Next, they are to copy the entry, its part of speech, and synonym list. Finally, the pupils are to create sample sentences for five of the synonyms.

C. Publishing Project:

1. The teacher will collect the portfolio work and assemble it into a class thesaurus of commonly overused terms. The class will refer to this booklet during the revision step of future writing assignments.

2. Computer Connection: Demonstrate the thesaurus option on the task bar of a word-processing program. Encourage the writers to explore this function when creating future compositions and reports.

IV. Evaluation

A. Use the discussion questions, practice exercises, and lesson worksheets to measure student progress and skill mastery.

B. Writing Applications: Use the four-point rubric scale to determine if students *can independently, can usually,* or *require assistance to* use the thesaurus to improve their vocabulary.

Thesaurus Power
Worksheet

*A **thesaurus** is a reference book that contains lists of synonyms and antonyms.*

> **road (n):** an open way for people or vehicles upon which to travel. *This <u>road</u> leads straight into downtown.*
>
> SYNONYMS:
>
> **alley:** a narrow road behind or between buildings. *This back door leads to a dark <u>alley</u>.*
>
> **boulevard:** a wide, main road, often lined with trees or separated with a grassy median strip. *The <u>boulevard</u> is decorated for the Fourth of July parade.*
>
> **highway:** a main road between cities. *Take this <u>highway</u> five miles south, and you will end up in Charleston.*
>
> **street:** a local road in a village or town, usually lined with sidewalks and houses. *Police headquarters is on the same <u>street</u> as the fire station.*
>
> **trail:** a narrow dirt or gravel trail through woods or unsettled regions. *Pioneer families took this <u>trail</u> west to the prairie lands.*
>
> **turnpike:** a public highway in which a toll is paid by travelers. *The next exit off the <u>turnpike</u> is twenty-four miles away.*
>
> ANTONYMS: blockade, cul-de-sac, dead end, detour.

Exercise A

Use the thesaurus entry above to answer the following questions.

1. What is the entry word above?

   _____

   _____

2. What part of speech is the entry and its synonyms?

   _____

   _____

3. Write the sample sentence for the entry word.

   _____

   _____

4. List all the synonyms.

   _____

   _____

5. List two more synonyms for this entry.

   _____

   _____

Thesaurus Power (cont.)
Worksheet

Exercise B

Complete each sentence with a different synonym for *road*. Write the sentence.

1. This _____ through the woods is too muddy to hike.

2. We stored a trash dumpster in the back _____.

3. The speed limit on one _____ is 70 miles per hour.

4. Memorial _____ was decorated with flags on every pole.

5. A new side _____ opened for two-way traffic.

Exercise C

Find the word *teach* in a thesaurus. Replace the word *teach* in the sentences below with a different synonym. Write each new sentence.

1. I can <u>teach</u> your dog to sit and stay.

   _____

2. My dad might <u>teach</u> soccer this fall.

   _____

3. College students have volunteered to help <u>teach</u> youngsters on the weekends.

   _____

   _____

4. <u>Teach</u> how this machine works.

   _____

5. A nurse can <u>teach</u> the class in first aid and CPR.

   _____

   _____

The Atlas and the Almanac

Students at the intermediate grade level use dictionaries and thesauruses daily to enrich their vocabularies. They also refer to encyclopedias for information on almost any topic. Intermediate studies expand from local events to those of national and international importance. The *atlas* and the *almanac* are two important reference sources these young people should become familiar with. This lesson is designed to give the students practice in gathering useful facts from both of these sources.

Goal:

Students will use atlases and almanacs as reference sources for expository writing.

Objectives:

1. Students examine an atlas and list five ways it differs from other reference sources.
2. Students examine an almanac and list five ways it differs from other reference sources.
3. Given a question, students will determine whether an atlas or almanac is the best reference source.

Materials:

- class set of atlases
- The Atlas and the Almanac Worksheet (pages 108 and 109)
- class set of almanacs
- Mapping Criteria Sheet (page 110)

Procedure:

I. Lesson Introduction

A. Ask volunteers to tell about the last time they used one of the following reference books. Have each volunteer explain an alternative plan of action if the book is not available. Inquire as to how they probably will use the books in the future.

   1. dictionary   3. telephone book

   2. encyclopedia   4. retail catalog

B. Introduce the atlas. Allow time for the students to examine its contents. Inform the students that this book of maps helps answer questions about specific places. Have them locate and note one example of the following:

   1. political map (human-made boundaries)

   2. physical map (nature's boundaries)

   3. other types of maps (product, road, climate, population, etc.)

C. Introduce the almanac. Allow time for the students to examine its contents. Inform them that this is a book of useful and interesting facts from the past and present. Have them locate and note one example of the following:

   1. a sports statistic

   2. a book, film, or music award winner

   3. the date of a solar eclipse

The Atlas and the Almanac *(cont.)*

II. Lesson Body

A. Compare and contrast the atlas and almanac.

    1. Together, create a list of at least five characteristics that make atlases and almanacs unique.

    2. Students are to generate suggestions for using an atlas and almanac for schoolwork or other activities in their day-to-day lives.

B. Distribute The Atlas and the Almanac worksheet. There are three activities that help students apply and practice the skills introduced during this lesson.

    1. The first exercise will help the teacher determine whether the students can distinguish between these two reference books. A question is presented, and the pupils must decide if an atlas or almanac is the better reference source.

    2. Atlas Application: After drilling and practicing the skills necessary for successful use of an atlas, students are asked to apply their mapping skills to create detailed maps of rooms in their houses. All the basic elements of a map are required plus a set of grid coordinates of significant areas. For best results, supply the students with graph paper for this project.

    3. Almanac Application: After drilling and practicing the skills necessary for successful use of an almanac, direct the students to the "perpetual calendar" feature. Students will be asked to make a list of significant dates in their family history and use the perpetual calendar to find out what day of the week these events took place.

III. Lesson Conclusion

A. Students are to restate the definitions of an atlas and an almanac, plus tell five characteristics that make each one of these reference books unique.

    1. *Atlas:* An atlas is a book of maps used to answer questions about the location of a specific place. Political, physical, product, climate, and population maps are commonly found in this reference book.

    2. *Almanac:* An almanac is a book of lists. Past and present events, statistics, important dates, scientific information, and historical facts are some of its useful data.

B. Writing Applications

    1. Instruct the students to pretend they are about to take a journey to a foreign country. Let them decide if it is a business trip or a vacation. Pupils are to use an almanac to research facts about the place they have chosen to visit. Information about the climate, culture, and the economy must be included in their reports. Direct the students to look under the heading "United States Customs" for information about foreign travel, duty, taxes, and passports.

    2. For a cover page, students are to draw maps of the foreign places described in their almanac report. Refer to the Mapping Criteria Sheet to determine the level of difficulty the students are to attempt.

IV. Evaluation

A. Use the discussion questions, practice exercises, and The Atlas and the Almanac lesson worksheet to measure student progress and mastery.

B. Writing Applications: Use the four-point rubric scale to determine if each student *can independently, can usually,* or *needs assistance to* use books to gather information for research topics.

The Atlas and the Almanac
Worksheet

An **atlas** *is a book of maps. Use it to answer questions about the locations of specific places.*
An **almanac** *is a book of lists. It is a handy, one-volume book used to quickly locate facts.*

Exercise A

Write the reference source you would use to answer each question. Choose *atlas* or *almanac*.

1. Who was the twentieth president of the United States? _____
2. What is a zip code for Houston, Texas?_____
3. Does the state of Washington have a border with Idaho? _____
4. Who is the current mayor of New York City? _____
5. How many telephone area codes does the city of Los Angeles have? _____
6. What interstate highway connects Columbus, Ohio, to Indianapolis, Indiana? _____
7. On what day of the year is Thanksgiving? _____
8. Where in Alaska is Point Barrow? _____
9. Which Wisconsin cities are on the shore of Lake Michigan?_____
10. What are the longitude and latitude of Cincinnati, Ohio?_____

Exercise B

Most almanacs have a feature entitled "Perpetual Calendar." These special calendars are used to discover the day of the week a specific date occurred in the past and will occur in the future. Make a list of five significant dates in your family history (birthdays, anniversaries, graduations, firsts, etc.) and use the perpetual calendar to find out what day of the week these events took place.

Date	Day of the Week
1.	
2.	
3.	
4.	
5.	

The Atlas and the Almanac
Worksheet *(cont.)*

Exercise C

Apply your mapping skills to create a detailed map of any room in your house. This map must have a title, key, compass rose, scale, and grid. Include an index that lists the coordinates of at least five significant areas of the room. Draw your map on graph below; then make it colorful.

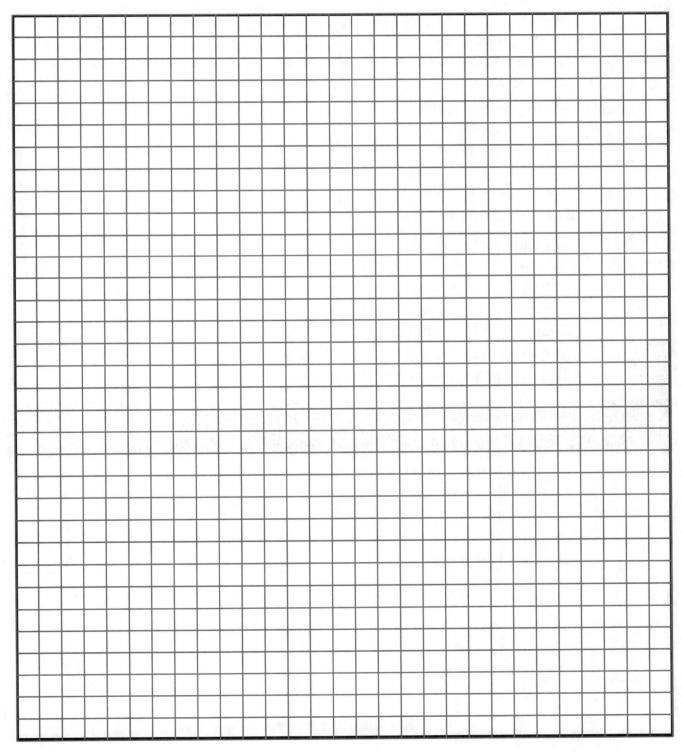

Mapping Criteria Sheet

Basic Project

The most basic maps created by the students should include the following:

- ❏ title
- ❏ map key or legend
- ❏ compass rose
- ❏ three cities
- ❏ two bodies of water
- ❏ one mountain chain
- ❏ farming, industry, and mining regions

Intermediate Project

This type of map requires the following elements:

- ❏ all the features of the basic map project
- ❏ scale
- ❏ three or more cities
- ❏ highways and roads
- ❏ specific lakes and rivers
- ❏ named mountains, hills, and valleys
- ❏ farming, industry, and mining regions

Challenge Project

This type of map requires the following elements:

- ❏ all the features of the basic and intermediate map projects
- ❏ a compass rose with intermediate directions
- ❏ a desert
- ❏ a harbor
- ❏ labeled tall mountain peaks
- ❏ dairy farm
- ❏ steel mill
- ❏ coal mine
- ❏ accurate scale
- ❏ appropriate coloring

Parts of a Book

Teachers will require intermediate students to use more than one source of information when research reports are assigned. Nonfiction books, encyclopedias, atlases, almanacs, and the Internet will be popular reference choices. The students will need a strategy to discover whether a book contains the necessary information to help them take notes and then compose their papers. This lesson is designed to introduce the four basic parts of a reference book that will help students determine if whether it is an appropriate source for their reports.

Goal:

Students will use a variety of nonfiction books as reference sources for expository writing.

Objectives:

1. Students will identify and list the basic elements of a title page, copyright page, table of contents, and index.
2. Students will use the title page, copyright page, table of contents, and index to locate information.

Materials:

- classroom textbooks (mathematics, science, health, social studies, etc.)
- reference books (atlas, almanac, dictionary, thesaurus, encyclopedia, etc.)
- 3" x 5" index cards.
- Parts of a Book worksheet (page 115)
- an old book from home

Procedure:

I. Lesson Introduction

A. Begin the class by having the students examine their textbooks. Make a chart. List titles, publishers, copyright dates, and on what pages the table of contents and index appear.

  1. Explain that the main part of the book is called the *body*. The body contains information arranged in units, chapters, topics, and subtopics.
  2. The other parts of the book are the *title page*, *copyright page*, *table of contents* (located towards the front of a book), and *index* (located towards the back of a book). These four parts give information about the makeup of a book, thus helping the reader to decide whether it will be appropriate and useful.

B. Explain the different parts and why these are important for successful research reporting. (These definitions are given on the Parts of a Book worksheet on page 113.)

Parts of a Book *(cont.)*

II. Lesson Body

A. Take a second look at the chart and the title pages, copyright pages, tables of contents, and indexes of the classroom textbooks. Give each student a 3" x 5" index card, and have them create a question (and answer) based upon information located on these pages. Collect the cards and play a round of "Twenty Questions," "Jeopardy!," or "Book Part Pursuit." Some sample questions follow:

  1. What book did Dr. James Bethal write? *(title page)*

  2. In what city is Veranos Press located? *(title card)*

  3. On what page does the chapter about Puzzles and Games begin? *(table of contents)*

  4. Is there a section about word problems? *(index)*

B. Distribute the Parts of a Book worksheet. On it students will find samples of a book's title page, copyright page, table of contents, and index. Written definitions of these are given on page 113.

  1. Exercise A asks the pupils to identify in what part of a book one would look to find several bibliographic bits of information.

  2. Exercise B requires the student to use parts of a given book to find exact answers to a series of questions.

III. Lesson Conclusion

A. Direct the students to review and recite the definitions of title page, copyright page, table of contents, and index. They also must tell their location in a given book.

B. Examine other reference, nonfiction, and fiction books found in the classroom.

  1. Compare and contrast copyright dates, publishers, and contents.

  2. Start a card file of this information to use as a quick reference in the future.

C. Writing Application

  1. Ask the students to each locate the oldest book in their home. Have them copy down the title, author, publisher, copyright date, and any other vital information about the book's makeup. Direct them to investigate and write a short history of how this antique book came into the family's possession.

  2. Publishing: Create a classroom showcase in which to display these old books and their descriptions. Appoint a student to be the curator and have him offer brief tours and explanations of the exhibit.

IV. Evaluation

A. Use the discussion questions, practice exercises, and Parts of a Book worksheet to measure student progress and mastery.

B. Writing Applications: Use the four-point rubric scale to determine if each student *can independently, can usually,* or *needs assistance to* use books to gather information for research topics.

Parts of a Book *(cont.)*

*The main part of a book is called the **body**. It presents main ideas, subtopics, and details in text, illustrations, photographs, maps, charts, graphs, and other visuals. Books have four other parts that offer meaningful information. These are the **title page**, **copyright page**, **table of contents**, and the **index**.*

Study the parts of the book on this page. Notice what information is presented on each page. Also, note which pages are located towards the front of the book and which are toward the back.

Title Page

Located in the front of a book, it contains the title, author, publisher, and place of publication.

Copyright Page

Located in the front of the book, it contains the date of publication and the publisher's name.

Table of Contents

Located in the front of the book, it contains the titles of units, chapters, and sections, along with page numbers.

Index

Located at the back of the book, it is an alphabetical listing of topics presented in the book. Subtopics and cross references to other listings can be found in the index.

See page 114 for an example of each type of page.

Parts of a Book *(cont.)*

Title Page

Mental
Math
Power

by Dr. James Bethal

Veranos Press
Painesville, OH

Copyright Page

© 2001 by Veranos Press

Table of Contents

CHAPTER	PAGE
1) Basic Math Facts	1
2) Fractions and Decimals	19
3) Order of Operations	47
4) Puzzles and Games	76

Index

five-step strategy 90–95, 145

problem solving 89–150

properties 200–225

   associative 210–215

   commutative 202–209

   distributive 216–220

properties of one 202, 210, 216

properties of zero 201

two-part questions 96–110, 146
see also: word problems

Parts of a Book
Worksheet

Exercise A

Identify which part of a book you would look at to gather the following information.

1. the book's author _____

2. on what page chapter 7 begins _____

3. when the book was published _____

4. whether the book lists any cross references _____

5. the pages in the book about problem solving _____

Exercise B

Use page 114 to answer the following questions.

6. Who wrote *Mental Math Power*?

   _____

   _____

7. In what year was this book published?

   _____

   _____

8. How many pages is the chapter on fractions and decimals?

   _____

   _____

9. On what pages will you find information about two-part questions?

   _____

   _____

10. Where can you look for information about problem solving?

   _____

   _____

Skimming and Scanning

Our 21st-century media centers are well-stocked with books, periodicals, audiovisual kits, and computer software. Teachers encourage their students to sample all this material and use it for research and written reports. With so much information and so many choices available, a youngster can easily be overwhelmed. Instead of searching for and reading items from these tall, vast stacks, the average student often refers to an encyclopedia as his or her only source for facts and figures. This lesson is designed to teach students to adjust their reading and retrieval rates. It introduces and offers practice with skimming and scanning, techniques that help a student locate information quickly.

Goal:

The students will use skimming and scanning to gather information for expository writing.

Objectives:

1. Students will use a skimming strategy to identify and recall the main ideas and details of a given reading selection.

2. Students will use a scanning strategy to locate and recall specific topics, key terms, and vocabulary in a given reading selection.

Materials:

- newspapers and periodicals
- Skimming and Scanning worksheet (pages 119 and 120)
- Book Report Form (page 122)

Procedure:

I. Lesson Introduction

A. Write the following terms on the chalkboard. Ask the students to list the different types of information each one of these sources can supply its user. Have volunteers give reasons why a person might not finish viewing, reading, or listening to a program, written article, or broadcast all the way to the end.

❏ newspapers and magazines   ❏ atlas
❏ television program   ❏ almanac
❏ radio broadcast   ❏ encyclopedia

Skimming and Scanning *(cont.)*

B. Introduce the term *skimming*. Skimming is a way of reading quickly to find out the main ideas and details of a piece of writing. There are three steps to this method of locating information quickly:

   1. Read the first paragraph completely and carefully.

   2. Read the first sentence or two of the remaining paragraphs.

   3. Read the last paragraph completely and carefully.

C. Introduce the term *scanning*. Scanning is searching the text quickly to locate a name, place, date, vocabulary word, or other key term. There are four steps to this method of locating information quickly:

   1. Skim the article.

   2. Identify a name, place, date, vocabulary word, or key term.

   3. Look over (scan) the text to locate the sentence in which it occurs.

   4. Read the entire sentence carefully to be sure the sentence includes the necessary information.

D. Inform the students that skimming and scanning are for times when it is not necessary to read all of a piece of writing. This strategy is best employed when one needs a general overview of the main ideas and important details or when one needs to find a particular bit of information. Some basic applications of this skill include the following:

   ❏ surveying unfamiliar text

   ❏ recalling and reviewing information

   ❏ outlining main ideas and details

   ❏ studying in preparation for tests

II. Lesson Body

A. Distribute the Skimming and Scanning worksheet. Restate the three steps for skimming and the four steps for scanning. Next, guide the students through the process and have them answer the practice questions on the worksheet.

   1. Read the first paragraph all the way through.

   2. Read the first sentences of the remaining paragraphs and note any headings, key terms, or new vocabulary related to the topic.

   3. Go on to the skimming practice questions.

   4. Reread the title and headings.

   5. Go on to the scanning practice questions.

Skimming and Scanning *(cont.)*

B. After the guided practice is complete, have the students try out these skills with articles from current newspapers and magazines. Instruct them to skim through a periodical for a headline or title that interests them. On a separate piece of paper, ask the pupils to note and then share the following information:

❑ the article's headline or title

❑ the main idea and four details

❑ any important names, places, dates, etc.

❑ why this particular story was of interest

III. Lesson Conclusion

A. Students will define the terms *skimming* and *scanning* and list possible applications of these skills. Review the proper way and appropriate places to use this technique. Inform the students that skimming and scanning are helpful when searching for information sources, especially in libraries or on the Internet, where the amount of material and choices are enormous and growing every day.

B. Writing Application: Direct the students to bring a fiction book to class, one that they have read but not recently. On a given day, review the skimming and scanning strategy and have students fill out the book report form that accompanies this lesson. Limit the time students have to complete the work and then discuss how this activity can be applied to other assignments or reading-proficiency exams.

C. Publishing: Have volunteers create a poster that lists the three steps to use when skimming an article and the four steps to use while scanning. Decorate it with current event articles and display in a visible place.

D. Computer Connection: Locate the e-mail addresses of the periodicals used for skimming and scanning practice during this lesson. Students are to go back to the articles they chose, reread them carefully, then send a message to the editor that expresses an opinion about that particular story.

IV. Evaluation

A. Use the discussion questions, practice exercises, and the Skimming and Scanning lesson worksheet to measure student progress and mastery.

B. Writing Applications: Use the four-point rubric scale to determine if each student *can independently, can usually,* or *needs assistance to* use books and other resources to gather information for research topics.

Skimming and Scanning
Worksheet

Skim this article about mummies. Remember to read the title and the headings. Take note of any key words, names, places, and dates. Then, complete the worksheet on the following page.

The Mummies of South America

An Incredible Discovery

When a person hears the word "mummy," he or she most often has visions of Ancient Egypt, pyramids, and royalty. Few people think about the ancient Indian empires of the western hemisphere. During the past year, a team of scientists led by Johan Reihard has made an incredible discovery. While exploring ancient ruins in South America, they uncovered three mummified bodies in near-perfect condition.

The Inca Indians

The Inca Indians were a wealthy civilization of people who ruled an empire in western South America. Inca lands stretched 2,500 miles down the coast from Columbia in the north to Chile in the south. They built cities throughout the Andes Mountains and were successful farmers, artists, and musicians. Their culture is known for its massive stone temples, arts and crafts, and their well-run government. The Inca nation thrived for hundreds of years until invading European settlers took control of the land.

Two Girls and One Boy

Underneath five feet of dry rock and earth lay the bodies of three adolescent Incas. Unlike other mummies, these were not freeze-dried without any soft tissue or blood. The two girls and one boy were simply frozen and still had intact organs and blood in their veins. Doctor Reihard and his team found the mummies during an expedition to the ruins in northern Argentina.

Secrets of the Mummies

Scientists are anxious to study these mummies. They expect to discover information about the diet, health, and origin of the Inca people. Clues to ancient rituals and religious practices may also be revealed. It is hoped that by examining these mummies, scientists will learn answers to the many unsolved mysteries of the Incas.

Skimming and Scanning (cont.)
Worksheet

Skimming Practice

1. Write the title and paragraph headings of the article on page 119.

   _____

   _____

   _____

2. What is this article's main idea?

   _____

   _____

   _____

   _____

Scanning Practice

Find the section of the article on page 119 that is related to the topic of each question. Look for key words, names, places, and dates. Remember to read the complete sentence when you think you have found the answer.

3. Where were the mummies buried?

   _____

   _____

4. Where were the Inca lands?

   _____

   _____

5. In what South American country were the mummies found?

   _____

   _____

6. What information do the scientists expect to discover?

   _____

   _____

Creating Reports

Book Report Form

Title: _____

Author: _____

Main Characters:_____

_____

Minor Characters: _____

_____

Setting (time and place):_____

_____

What lesson was the story trying to teach? _____

_____

_____

The part I liked best was_____

_____

_____

The part I did not like was _____

_____

_____

Others SHOULD or SHOULD NOT read this story because _____

_____

_____

_____

Signature _____

Date Submitted _____

Outrageous Outlines

Once the students have learned how to use encyclopedias, atlases, almanacs, and a variety of other reference sources to gather facts and figures about a topic, the next step is to organize this information in a meaningful way. An outline helps pupils remember and understand what has been read and researched. Outlining is a crucial skill, necessary for successful expository writing. It also aids a student in recalling and applying this newly discovered knowledge while taking tests. This lesson is designed to teach pupils correct outlining techniques, a procedure vital for the preparation of a research report.

Goal:

The students will apply outlining skills to organize their expository writing.

Objectives:

1. Students will identify the basic elements of an outline and describe their purposes.
2. Given a short article, students will identify its main topics, subtopics, and details in order to create an outline.

Materials:

- sample outline
- Outrageous Outlines Worksheets #1, #2, and #3 (pages 127–131)

Procedure:

I. Lesson Introduction

A. Instruct a small group of students to improvise and play-act a scene in which a teacher has assigned a report about "The Uses of the Peanut." The setting is a library/media center, the characters can be students, librarians, and teachers; and the plot will describe how the pupils go about gathering information on this topic.

1. Encourage the actors to use a bit of humor but to stay on the topic of gathering information for their report.
2. The last line of the skit should be something like, "Now that we have found all these books, magazines, and Web sites, how are we going to organize it?"

Outrageous Outlines *(cont.)*

    B. After the small group has performed their play, distribute the sample outline. Direct the students' attention to its basic parts and format and describe each one and its function.

        1. Basic Elements:

            a. Main Topics: titles, headings, and main-idea sentences

            b. Subtopics: questions an article answers that clarify the main topic

            c. Details: information that clarifies and expands upon the subtopics

    C. Use the title, main topics, subtopics, and details from the sample outline to create an expository paragraph about the uses of the peanut.

        1. Turn the outline's title into a topic sentence.

        2. Organize the subtopics into supporting sentences.

        3. Use the details to make the supporting sentences more descriptive.

        4. Conclude with a summary statement.

        5. Ask a volunteer to recite the completed composition.

II. Lesson Body

    A. State that outlining is a very useful technique for organizing information. A quality outline will also help a person remember and comprehend what has been read and researched.

        1. Intermediate, middle grade, high school, and college students often outline the chapters of books they are studying.

        2. People who give speeches and oral reports often outline the main ideas and details on index cards and then refer to them during their talks.

        3. Teachers' lesson plans are sometimes organized in the form of an outline.

        4. Ask the class to brainstorm other uses for outlining (e.g., shopping lists, construction procedures, a book's table of contents, television-program guides, etc.)

    B. Give each child a copy of the Outrageous Outlines Worksheet #1. Direct them to skim the article for main ideas and details. Tell them to scan the text for names, places, dates, and other terms that relate to the title. After that, instruct the students to think of questions they expect the article to answer.

        1. Guide the pupils through this activity.

        2. Complete the outline by using the main ideas, subtopics, and details listed at the end of the lesson.

Outrageous Outlines *(cont.)*

C. Use the Outrageous Outlines Worksheet #2 for review and extended practice. For those students who are struggling, guide them once again. For those who are on their way towards mastery, let them work quietly on their own.

    1. For Roman numerals I and II, ask for main ideas, subtopics, and details and have students identify what to write on the lines.

    2. For Roman numerals III and IV, state an item and have the students identify it as a main topic, subtopic, or detail; and then tell its correct line placement.

III. Lesson Conclusion

A. Summarize the main points of the lesson. Refer back to the sample outline and lesson worksheets and ask students to name the parts and describe the format. Make a list of the purpose of outlining.

    1. organize information

    2. remember and understand what has been read

    3. discover how important details are related

    4. use as a note-taking strategy

    5. use as a test-taking study guide

B. Writing Application

    1. Have the pupils make an outline of the years they have spent in school (page 127). Grades, teachers' names, friends, and one important memory will serve as main topics, subtopics, and details. Use the guide on the following page for placing information.

    2. Publishing: Ask the students to bring in yearbooks or scrapbooks from these school years. Schedule time for the pupils to share their outlines, memories, pictures, and artifacts.

C. Computer Connection: Demonstrate how to use a CD-ROM encyclopedia to gather information for research reports. Direct them to the outline feature that accompanies most of the encyclopedia entries. Some word-processing programs also have an outlining template. Instruct the students to try this feature and apply its functions to future assignments.

IV. Evaluation

A. Use the discussion questions, practice exercises, and the Outrageous Outlines Worksheets to measure student progress and mastery.

B. Writing Applications: Use the four-point rubric scale to determine if each student *can independently, can usually,* or *needs assistance to* use an outline to organize researched information.

Outrageous Outlines
Sample Outline

The Many Uses of the Peanut

I. Peanuts are useful for food.

  A. Peanuts are roasted in the shell.

      1. Shelled peanuts are eaten as a snack.

      2. Shelled peanuts are used as a flavoring in recipes.

  B. Peanut oil is extracted.

      1. Peanut oil is used for frying.

      2. Peanut oil is used as vegetable shortening.

  C. Peanuts can be ground into peanut butter.

II. Peanuts are useful on a farm.

  A. Peanut shells are added to fertilizer.

  B. Peanut plants are recycled.

      1. They are reused as animal bedding.

      2. They are reused and plowed into fields as an additional soil nutrient.

III. Peanuts are useful as other products.

  A. In industry:

      1. Peanut oil is used to lubricate machinery.

      2. Peanut powder is used as an additive in plastic and glue.

  B. At home:

      1. Peanuts are ingredients in personal care products.

      2. Some soaps, face powders, and shaving creams contain peanuts.

Sample Paragraph

Do you know how many ways there are to use peanuts? They are most often eaten as food. People munch on them as snacks or add peanuts to cookies, cakes, and breads. However, peanuts have many other uses, too. Farmers mix peanut shells into fertilizers and sometimes recycle the rest of the plant as bedding in their animal barns. Peanut oil can be applied as a lubricant, and ground-up peanuts are found in plastics, glue, and soap. Now you know a number of uses for the peanut.

Outrageous Outlines
Worksheet #1

My First Four Years in Public School

I. Kindergarten
    A. My teacher was Mrs. Knott.
    B. My friends
        1. Ronnie Combo
        2. Mark Gordon
        3. Denise Skerl
    C. My favorite memories
        1. Making robots out of construction paper at the art table
        2. Marching in the "Turn Off the TV" parade through our town

II. First Grade
    A. My teacher was _____
    B. My friends
        1. _____
        2. _____
        3. _____
    C. My favorite memories
        1. _____
        2. _____

III. Second Grade
    A. _____
    B. _____
        1. _____
        2. _____
        3. _____
    C. _____
        1. _____
        2. _____

IV. _____
    A. _____
    B. _____
        1. _____
        2. _____
        3. _____
    C. _____
        1. _____
            _____
        2. _____
            _____

Outrageous Outlines
Worksheet #2

Read the following article about Canada's Inuit people and their new territory. Think about its main ideas, subtopics, and details. Complete the outline on the following page by using the items listed in the Outline Box. Several spaces have already been filled in for you.

A New Northern Neighbor

Nunavut (nu-na-voot) was born on April 1, 1999. It is not a person or beast but a new territory of the country of Canada. Nunavut covers 733,587 square miles of arctic tundra and islands from the Hudson Bay in the south all the way to the top of the world. Before its creation, it was part of Canada's Northwest Territories.

A majority of the people who live in Nunavut are of Inuit descent. Their language is called Inuktitut, and most of these natives write in syllabics, or signs that represent word sounds. The Inuit people depend on the fishing and mining industry for work. They are also known for their fine arts and crafts. Inuits control most of the new legislative offices in Nunavut.

Nunavut's leaders plan to build a better future for their children. The Canadian National Government has budgeted hundreds of millions of dollars to improve the area's education, health, and social services. With better schools and training, it is hoped that more Inuit adults will find regular employment. The people of Nunavut have been neglected in the past. Canada is trying to correct these mistakes by giving Inuits back their land and money to manage it.

Nunavut

Outrageous Outlines
Worksheet #2 *(cont.)*
A New Northern Neighbor

I. Nunavut

   A. April 1, 1999

   B. _____

      1. _____

      2. _____

II. _____

   A. Language

      1. _____

      2. _____

   B. _____

      1. Fishing

      2. Mining

      3. _____

III. Nunavut's future

   A. _____

      1. _____

      2. _____

   B. Correcting the mistakes of the past

      1. _____

      2. _____

Outline Box

- Inuktitut

- Arts and crafts

- 733,587 square miles

- Money to manage the land

- New territory of Canada

- Economy

- Syllabics

- Giving back Inuits their land

- Improve education, health, and social services

- Spans from Hudson Bay to the top of the world

- More adults find regular jobs

- Building a better life for their children

- Natives are of Inuit descent.

Outrageous Outlines
Worksheet #3

Read the following article about young people and their drinking of soda pop. Think about its main ideas, subtopics, and details. Complete the outline (page 131) by using the items listed in the Outline Box. Several spaces have already been filled in for you.

Soft Drinks, Students, and Sugar

Soft drinks are more popular than ever. Today, young people drink twice as much soda pop as they did 20 years ago. Back then, the children were only served pop as a special treat at parties and picnics. Now, it is common to drink soda at breakfast, lunch, and dinner.

Most of these beverages contain little or no vitamins or minerals. A 12-ounce can contains 10 teaspoonfuls of sugar. The average teenage boy ingests 15 teaspoonfuls of sugar every day, while the average teenage girl swallows 10 teaspoonfuls of sugar in the form of soft drinks. Health experts are worried about all this poor nutrition among young people.

America's schools are making lots of money from the sale of soft drinks. Vending machines have been placed in many elementary, middle, and high school buildings. Schools use the profits from soda sales to purchase books, computers, uniforms, and other needed supplies.

Not everyone believes that the selling of soft drinks in school is a good idea. Many doctors are upset that school officials and politicians are encouraging the students and their teachers to buy more. Most students like the fact that pop is available at school, but they will also admit that sometimes they eat too much sugar. Are soft drinks for sale in your school?

Outrageous Outlines
Worksheet #3 *(cont.)*

Soft Drinks, Students, and Sugar

I. Soft drinks are more popular than ever.

  A. _____

     1. _____

     2. _____

  B. Today

     1. _____

     2. _____

II. Little or no vitamins or minerals

  A. _____

     1. _____

     2. _____

     3. Teenage girls ingest 10 teaspoonfuls a day.

  B. _____

III. _____

  A. Making lots of money

  B. _____

  C. _____

     1. _____

     2. _____

IV. Not everyone believes it is a good or bad idea.

  A. _____

  B. Officials encourage more soft drink sales.

     1. _____

     2. _____

  C. _____

     1. _____

     2. _____

Outline Box

- Special treat
- Ten teaspoonfuls in a 12-ounce can
- Doctors are upset.
- How schools are using the profits
- Twenty years ago
- Teachers encouraged to buy more soft drinks
- Vending machines in school buildings
- Student reactions
- Breakfast, lunch, and dinner
- Students encouraged to buy more soft drinks
- Teenage boys ingest 15 teaspoonfuls of sugar a day.
- Young people drink twice as much.
- Parties and picnics
- Health experts are worried.
- Books, computers, and uniforms
- They eat too much sugar.
- Other needed supplies
- America's Schools
- They like the availability of soft drinks.
- Sugar

Standards and Benchmarks: 1A, 1B, 1C, 1D, 1E, 1F, 1G, 2A, 2B, 2C, 3A, 3B, 3C, 3D, 3E, 3F, 3G, 3H, 3I, 3J, 3K, 3L, 4A, 4B, 4C, 4D, 4G

The Research Report

A research paper is one of the most difficult tasks assigned to young writers. First, students are directed to report on a topic about which they know little. Then, besides writing, this project requires an application of many higher-level thinking skills to produce the final composition. The prewriting step is much more involved, and pupils will have to decide what to write about; what to tell; where to look for information; and how to organize the notes, facts, and figures. A strong effort must be made while researching and planning—otherwise the writing and revising will be a slow process. This lesson is designed to guide the learners step by step to produce a three-paragraph report.

Goal:

The students will prewrite, write, revise, and publish a three-paragraph research report.

Objectives:

1. The students will identify a school or community problem or concern and then research what is being done to solve it.

2. After identifying the school or community problem or concern, students will state their opinion and support them with facts.

Materials:

- sample research report (page 136)
- library reference materials
- index cards or notebook

Procedure:

I. Lesson Introduction

A. Inform the students that they are about to begin a writing project that is more involved than basic paragraph writing. It will be necessary to use a variety of skills to produce the final copy. They will have to spend time in the library and schedule interviews with other students and adults to gather information. After that, the paper will have to be organized in a specific way. The finished work will be shared with the class. This same procedure will be used numerous times in other subjects during their intermediate, middle grade, and high school years.

B. The purpose of this report is to identify a school or community problem, explain what has been done to solve it, express an opinion, and offer a constructive suggestion about the entire matter. The project will be more enjoyable if the pupils choose topics that are of personal interest or concern. Topics need to be narrowed. For example, instead of writing about "School Vandalism," a better topic might be "Graffiti" or "Damage to Locker Rooms."

The Research Report *(cont.)*

C. After a narrowed topic has been decided upon, students will create thesis sentences. This will serve as the paper's main idea. Pupils will write it down in their notes or on an index card and refer to it as they look for background information about it. Often this statement will change or be modified as the project progresses. The following is a list of topics to share with the students. Have them practice creating thesis sentences with these topics.

1. school uniforms
2. taking proficiency tests
3. classroom size

4. urban sprawl into rural areas
5. traffic problems and dangers
6. recreation opportunities

D. The students will use their thesis statements to generate a series of questions to research and answer in their papers.

1. The first paragraph will define the problem. (*What is the problem? Who is affected? When and where does it happen?*)

2. The second paragraph will describe the problem's consequences and what has been done to solve it. (*Why is this happening? What has been done to stop it? Who do I talk to about it?*)

3. The last paragraph will express the student's reaction, opinion, and suggestions to improve the situation. (*What do I think about this? What has been done to solve it? What can we do?*)

These questions and answers will serve as subtopics and details which relate to the main topic. They will also give the pupils ideas of where to start to look for facts, figures, and further input.

E. Once the thesis statement and subtopics have been recorded, it is time for the students to begin their research. It is best that they look for recently published material. Since students will be reading, hearing, and sharing opinions about their topics, some review, drill, and practice distinguishing *fact* from *opinion* may be necessary.

1. For school-related topics, district newsletters; students newspapers; and interviews with principals, teachers, students, parents, and custodians may be useful. Students might be directed to use the Internet to discover how other schools and students are dealing with similar problems.

2. For community-related topics, local newspapers, editorials, minutes of city council meetings, public hearings, and interviews with local officials and concerned groups will be informative. Students could use the Internet to locate their community's Web site and discover if their topic is mentioned there.

F. Share the following researching tips with the class.

1. It is crucial to carefully take notes on index cards or in a reporter's notebook. Double-check everything that is written down, and make sure the source is noted in case it is necessary to go back to it later—especially if a bibliography is required as part of the report.

2. Students need to organize their research in an outline. The main idea or thesis statement will describe the problem the paper is about. The subtopics and details of the first paragraph will list who is involved plus where and when it occurs. The second section's main idea describes why the problem is happening, and its subtopics and details list exactly what is being done to address it. The last section expresses the writer's opinion and suggestions. The subtopics and details list facts that support the student's point of view.

The Research Report *(cont.)*

II. Lesson Body

A. Students are to use their notes and outlines to create the rough draft. The thesis statement begins the paper, and then the subtopics and details serve as supporting sentences. Use the second main topic from the outline to begin the second paragraph. Add supporting sentences and repeat this procedure once again for the final paragraph. If you require the students to have a bibliography, that goes at the end. Finally, direct the pupils to give their compositions attractive, informative titles.

B. Schedule time for the students to read their rough drafts to an audience. Place a box or small platform in front of the class and call for volunteers to "stand up and sound off." Solicit from the listeners suggestions that will help the writers improve their reports and make their messages clear. Restate that any personal opinions expressed in the final paragraphs must be supported with facts uncovered during their research.

C. Direct the students to proofread for errors in capitalization, punctuation, spelling, and grammar. Pupils need to affirm that the composition follows the outline, each paragraph begins with a topic sentence, and researched information is paraphrased and written in the writer's own words.

III. Lesson Conclusion

A. Students are to make a legible copies of their reports. Encourage them to use a word-processing program if one is available. A bibliographic list of sources is a good topic to discuss and include at the end of the report (page 135).

   1. Explain how to correctly list reference sources in a bibliography and discuss the purpose of footnotes. Show a few examples in textbooks and other materials.

   2. Direct advanced writers to use features such as spell checkers and to experiment with different fonts as they create their final copies on the computer.

B. A picture tells a thousand words. Students can make a photo essay or videotape to accompany their reports. Still pictures can be mounted and labeled describing the problems the students wrote about. A videotape can capture the student's narration as the camera pans the problem areas.

C. Computer Connection: For school-related topics, students could e-mail their final copies to the superintendent or a school board member. For community concerns, the mayor's office or a city council representative might be interested in reading the thoughts of the local young people.

D. To conclude the lesson, review the process to follow when assigned a research report. Restate the purposes for choosing an interesting topic, writing a thesis statement, good planning, and thorough research. Ask the pupils to list other subjects for which future research reporting will be required. Also, relate this type of writing to careers and life outside of school.

IV. Evaluation

A. Use the student's thesis statement, research notes, and outlines to measure progress and mastery.

B. Writing Application: Use the four-point rubric scale to determine if students *can independently, can usually,* or *require assistance to* write research reports.

How to Write a Bibliography

The importance of accurately citing resources used when writing a research report cannot be overstated. It is absolutely necessary. The basic rules for citing resources are as follows:

- Always write the author's last name first (followed by a comma), then the first name. If there is more than one author of the work, write the first author's last name first (followed by a comma), then the first name, and then list the rest of the authors.

- Begin the first line of an entry on the left margin of the page, then indent ½ inch for the remaining lines of that entry.

- Double-space all entries.

- Capitalize the first letter of each word in titles.

- Underline (or italicize, if using a computer) the names of books, journals, magazines, newspapers, and films.

Below are the basic ways to cite resources in your bibliography.

Book

Epstein, Norrie. *The Friendly Shakespeare*. Viking Press, New York, 1993.

Part of a Book
(such as an essay or an article from a collection of articles)

Feynman, Richard P. "Atoms in Motion." *The World Treasury of Physics, Astronomy, and Mathematics*. Edited by Timothy Ferries. United States of America, 1991. Pages 3–17.

Article in a Periodical
(such as a newspaper or magazine)

Cox, Beverly and Martin Jacobs. "Spirit of the Harvest." *Native People Magazine*. Volume 10, Number 2 (1997): Pages 12–17.

Web Page

Nigro, Frank G. *Franxfiles*. Revised 18 January 1999. 21 June 1999.
http://shastacollege.edu/english/fnigro/

The Research Report
Sample Composition

Too Much Graffiti

There has been a noticeable increase in the amount of graffiti around our school. At first you saw it written only on desks and chairs. Now it is being scribbled on restroom walls, locker doors, and many other places. The graffiti is mostly the names of girls, boys, and music groups; but some of the words are very vulgar. Students are using permanent ink, which is difficult to clean off and remove. This graffiti is ruining the appearance of our school.

The principals and teachers have tried several plans to stop this type of vandalism. Classrooms have been assigned a designated restroom time and area. Teachers are to inspect the lavatories more closely and more often. Students caught defacing our school now face stiffer penalties. As in the past, offenders serve a detention. Now they must also come in on a Saturday and clean off the marks. However, these ideas may not be enough to stop this crime.

Our school should try one of the methods another school used to fight vandalism and graffiti. We need to have an assembly to boost school pride. Holbrook Intermediate School in Painesville, Ohio, did this—and it worked. The school band played, the choir sang, sports teams were introduced, and outstanding students were recognized. A guest speaker came and gave Holbrook's students a pep talk, and they all returned to class with a renewed sense of pride in their school. The punishments for damaging our school are necessary, but the spread of positive feelings will also help us take better care of the building, books, and each other. Let us cheer instead of smear!

Answer
Key

Answer Key

What Is Expository Writing?

Page 24—Worksheet #1

Answers will vary.

Page 25—Worksheet #2

Exercise A

1. nonfiction
2. nonfiction
3. fiction
4. nonfiction
5. fiction
6. fiction
7. nonfiction
8. fiction
9. fiction
10. nonfiction

Exercise B

1. Instructional
2. Informative

Page 26—Worksheet #3

Exercise A

1. nonfiction
2. nonfiction
3. fiction
4. fiction
5. nonfiction
6. fiction
7. nonfiction

Page 27—Exercise B

1. The correct sentence sequence is: 3, 5, 2, 4, 1.
2. instructional

The Writing Process

Page 31—Worksheet #1

Exercise A

1. D
2. A
3. C
4. B

Exercise B

1. prewriting
2. publishing
3. revising
4. writing
5. publishing
6. prewriting
7. writing
8. revising

Page 32—Worksheet #2

Exercise A

1. Prewriting: A writer discovers and develops an idea.
2. Writing: Put ideas down on paper for the first time.
3. Revising: Edit, proofread, and make changes.
4. Publishing: Share the final composition with others.

Exercise B

Use the four-point rubric scale to evaluate the students' thank-you notes.

Paragraph Perfection

Page 36—Worksheet #1

Exercise A

1. Yes
2. Yes
3. No
4. Yes

Answer Key *(cont.)*

5. Yes

6. No

7. No

8. Yes

9. Yes

Exercise B

1. The correct sentence sequence is: 3, 2, 6, 5, 1, 4.

2. Sentence number 3 should be underlined once, and sentence number 4 should be underlined twice.

Page 37—Worksheet #2

Exercise A

1. Yes

2. Yes

3. No

4. Yes

5. No

6. No

Exercise B

The correct sentence sequence is: 5, 2, 3, 4, 1.

Exercise C

1. Main idea sentence: There are many things to do at a county fair.

2. Cross out: The Ferris wheel is my favorite ride.

Terrific Topic Sentences

Page 43—Worksheet #2

Exercise A

Answers will vary.

Exercise B

Answers will vary.

Thesaurus Power

Superb Summaries

Page 47—Worksheet #1

Exercise A

Cross out: People often take rides in hot air balloons at carnivals.

Exercise B

1. Main idea: On March 21, 1999, Bertrand Piccard and Brian Jones became the first humans to complete a nonstop trip around the world in a balloon.

   Conclusion: Skill, state-of-the-art equipment, and good luck were all necessary for Piccard and Jones to make aviation history in a balloon.

2. Answers will vary.

3. Answers will vary.

Pages 48 and 49—Worksheet #2

Exercise A

Answers will vary.

Exercise B

The topic and conclusion sentences will vary, but the paragraph must be proofread for proper capitalization, punctuation, spelling, grammar, and legibility.

Nifty Nouns

Page 53—Worksheet

Exercise A

(possible answers)

1. hour

2. mystery

3. museum

4. nuts and bolts

5. vegetables, salt, and pepper

Answer Key *(cont.)*

Exercise B

(nouns to replace)

1. relative
2. types, metals
3. country, countries
4. people, animals
5. relative, place

Vivid Verbs

Page 54—Worksheet

Exercise A

(possible answers)

1. sprinted
2. enjoys
3. fire
4. repeat
5. devoured

Exercise B

(verbs to replace)

1. go
2. sit, put on
3. start
4. rolls
5. are

Adjective Attention

Page 57—Worksheet

Exercise A

1. how many
2. what kind
3. how many
4. what kind
5. what kind
6. what kind
7. what kind
8. what kind
9. how many
10. what kind
11. how many
12. how many
13. what kind
14. how many
15. what kind
16. how many

Exercise B

1. how many
2. what kind, what kind
3. how many
4. what kind, what kind
5. young, old
6. only, pair
7. good, guide, helpful
8. experienced, powerful
9. quiet (what kind)
   wooded (what kind)
10. several (how many)
    curious (what kind)
11. different (what kind)
    small (what kind)
12. these (what kind)
    important (what kind)

Appealing Adverbs

Pages 60 and 61—Worksheet

Exercise A

1. brightly
2. carefully

Answer Key (cont.)

3. helplessly

4. roughly

5. quickly

6. curiously

7. finally

8. poorly

9. quietly

10. softly

11. courageously

12. harmfully

13. occasionally

14. selectively

15. successfully

Exercise B

1. wildly

2. loudly

3. quickly

4. hard

5. completely

6. carefully, use

7. often, flammable

8. outdoors, barbecue

9. responsibly, handle

10. rapidly, leave

11. always, follow

12. never, should hold

13. also, deadly

14. quickly, dial

15. never, play

Simile Spice

Page 65—Worksheet

Exercise A

Answers will vary.

Exercise B

11. a

12. c

Marvelous Metaphors

Page 70—Worksheet

Exercise A

Answers will vary.

Exercise B

11. b

12. c

Personification Metaphors

Page 74 and 75—Worksheet

Exercise A

1. c

2. b

3. a

4. a

5. c

6. b

7. a

8. a

Exercise B

Answers will vary.

The Explanatory Paragraph

Pages 81 and 82—Worksheet

Exercise A

1. First

2. Next

3. Then

4. After that

5. Finally

6. At last

Answer Key *(cont.)*

Exercise B

The correct sentence sequence is: 4, 6, 2, 1, 7, 5, 3.

Writing Directions

Page 87—Worksheet

Exercise A

1. Turn right at the next stoplight.
2. The arrow is pointing up.
3. Hiram Village is north from here.
4. Take the elevator down to the parking garage.
5. This store has plenty of parking in front.

Exercise B

Answers will vary.

The Cause-and-Effect Paragraph

Page 91 and 92—Worksheet #1

Exercise A

Answers will vary.

Exercise B

Answers will vary.

Page 93—Worksheet #2

1. c
2. c
3. Answers will vary.

The Contrast Paragraph

Page 96—Worksheet

Exercise A

1. difference
2. not
3. while
4. however
5. Unlike

6. or

Exercise B

1. different
2. unlike
3. In contrast
4. while
5. not the same

The Comparative Paragraph

Page 100—Worksheet

Exercise A

1. similar
2. Each
3. typical
4. both
5. also
6. in common

Exercise B

1. in common
2. similar
3. Also
4. both
5. Likewise
6. alike

Thesaurus Power

Page 104—Worksheet

Exercise A

1. road
2. noun
3. This road leads straight into downtown.
4. alley, boulevard, highway, street, trail, and turnpike
5. avenue, lane, etc.

Answer Key *(cont.)*

Page 105—Worksheet

Exercise B

1. path
2. alley
3. highway
4. Boulevard
5. street

Exercise C

1. train
2. coach
3. tutor
4. demonstrate
5. instruct

The Atlas and the Almanac

Page 108—Worksheet

Exercise A

1. almanac
2. almanac
3. atlas
4. almanac
5. almanac
6. atlas
7. almanac
8. atlas
9. atlas
10. atlas

Parts of a Book

Page 115—Worksheet

Exercise A

1. title page
2. table of contents
3. copyright page

4. index
5. index

Exercise B

6. Dr. James Bethal
7. 2001
8. about 27 pages
9. pages 96–110, 146
10. pages 89–150

Skimming and Scanning

Page 119—Worksheet

1. The Mummies of South America

    a. An Incredible Discovery

    b. The Inca Indians

    c. Two Girls and One Boy

    d. Secrets of the Mummies

2. The mummified bodies of ancient Indians have been found in South America. The mummies are in excellent shape, and scientists will be able to learn a great deal about life back in those times by studying them.

3. The mummies were buried in the ancient ruins of South America.

4. Inca lands were along South America's western coast. They went from Columbia in the north to Chile in the south.

5. The mummies were found in the Inca ruins of northern Argentina.

6. Scientists hope to answer many questions about Inca life, customs, and traditions.

Answer Key *(cont.)*

Outrageous Outlines

Pages 128 and 129—Worksheet #2

I. Nunavut

  A. April 1, 1999

  B. New territory of Canada

    1. 733,587 square miles

    2. Spans from Hudson Bay to the top of the world

II. Natives are of Inuit descent

  A. Language

    1. Inuktitut

    2. Syllabics

  B. Economy

    1. Fishing

    2. Mining

    3. Arts and Crafts

III. Nunavut's future

  A. Building a better life for their children

    1. Improve education, health, and social services

    2. More adults find regular jobs

  B. Correcting the mistakes of the past

    1. Giving back Inuits their land

    2. Money to manage the land

Pages 130 and 131—Worksheet #3

I. Soft drinks are more popular than ever.

  A. Twenty years ago

    1. Special treat

    2. Parties and picnics

  B. Today

    1. Young people drink twice as much.

    2. Breakfast, lunch, and dinner

II. Little or no vitamins or minerals

  A. Sugar

    1. Ten teaspoonfuls in a 12-ounce can

    2. Teenage boys ingest 15 teaspoonfuls of sugar a day.

    3. Teenage girls ingest 10 teaspoonfuls a day.

  B. Health experts are worried.

III. America's Schools

  A. Making lots of money

  B. Vending machines in the school buildings

  C. How schools are using the profits

    1. Books, computers, and uniforms

    2. Other needed supplies

IV. Not everyone believes it is a good or bad idea.

  A. Doctors are upset.

  B. Officials encourage more soft drink sales.

    1. Teachers encouraged to buy more soft drinks

    2. Students encouraged to buy more soft drinks

  C. Student Reactions

    1. They like the availability of soft drinks.

    2. They eat too much sugar.